Great Teaching With
GRAPHIC ORGANIZERS

Lessons and fun-shaped templates
that motivate kids of all learning styles

by Patti Drapeau

SCHOLASTIC
PROFESSIONAL BOOKS

NEW YORK · TORONTO · LONDON · AUCKLAND · SYDNEY
MEXICO CITY · NEW DELHI · HONG KONG

ACKNOWLEDGMENTS

I would like to express my appreciation to the teachers and students in Freeport, Maine, for their cooperation and support. Special thanks to the students who field tested many formats and helped to modify or design their own graphic organizers. The following students allowed their graphics and/or responses to be shared: Molly Lincoln, Danny Mehler, Daniel Soley, Kevin Gridley, Daniel Sandbeg, Jeff Smith, Nick Heinz, Elizabeth Geredien, Adam Cutler, and Katie Gray. Many thanks to the teachers at Morse Street School who allowed me to come into their classroom to do demonstration lessons as well as collect responses to be shared in this book. A thank you to Liza Moore the computer teacher at Mast Landing School who willingly formatted some of my hand drawn graphic organizers on the computer for me.

A thank you to the many graduate students I taught at the University of Southern Maine. They provided me with much needed feedback as they reviewed the different graphic organizers and also field tested them in their classrooms. A special thanks to Deborah Gott and Anne Rodier whose outstanding work is presented in this book in the section that discusses using the Drawing Conclusions Chart. A special thank you to Betsy Webb who transformed a graphic organizer into the butterfly design for me. A final thank you to James Curry, professor at the University of Southern Maine and coauthor of the Curry/Samara Model of Curriculum, Instruction, and Assessment, who introduced me to the idea of thinking skills charts.

DEDICATION

To my incredibly talented and creative husband Lenny, who is always a source of inspiration and provides me with much needed patience, guidance, and support. To my two wonderful daughters Kasey and Sara, who sacrifice their time with me in order to allow me to do what I need to do. To my mother and sister who I know are always there for me. To Roxie, the dog, who provides me with companionship while we take our walks in the woods. And to Natasha, the cat, who is our constant source of comic relief.

Front cover design by Kathy Massaro
Interior design by Solutions by Design, Inc.
Reproducible graphic organizers illustrated by Rusty Fletcher

ISBN 0-590-12876-0

Table of Contents

Introduction

Do you doodle while on the phone, draw pictures in your notebook during a lecture, or circle the most pressing item on your To-Do list? If so, you're using a graphic organizer, which is just a fancy term for doodles that help us highlight important ideas.

In the classroom, students use graphic organizers in much the same way that adults do—to stay focused and as an aid in organizing and comprehending information. Whether a student's organizer is a simple asterisk he jots in the margins to remember homework or a more formal forecasting chart like the one found in this book, the net effect is the same: The student is combining symbols and words to communicate ideas in a structured, precise way.

Two of the most common graphic organizers used in classrooms are Venn diagrams and brainstorming webs, as they provide a simple format for students to record their ideas.

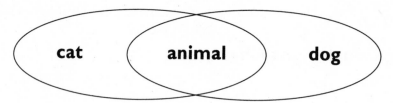

In the Venn diagram above, two different animals are identified. One animal, the *cat*, is written in one circle. The other animal, the *dog*, is written in the other circle. What they have in common is stated in the overlapping or center circle. In this case, they are both *animals*.

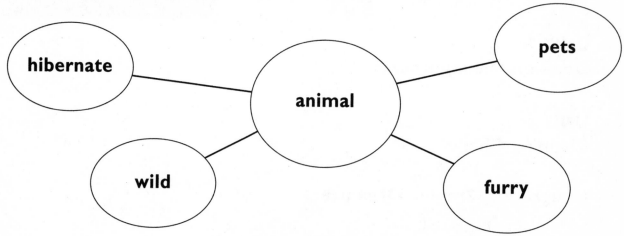

In the web above, students are asked to brainstorm things they know about animals. The word *animal* is placed in the center circle and the students free-associate what they know about this topic. Their ideas are placed in the spokes around the center circle.

Graphic organizers are teaching tools that appeal to all types of students. They help visual learners *see* what you are trying to convey and provide a structure that helps children with limited attention spans stay focused.

They are also outstanding assessment tools, providing you with a concise blueprint of a student's understanding of a concept and, in turn, of a student's ways of thinking. For example, you might ask students to use a Venn diagram to compare and contrast two characters in a story. The graphic organizer will show you what the students know and remember about the characters, and clue you in on their grasp of a story's meaning.

As educators, we're encouraged to integrate content and not teach subjects in isolation. A graphic organizer enables us to show and explain relationships between content and sub-content and how they in turn relate to other content areas. For example, when brainstorming about our community, we can ask students to relate community to family members, helpers, and leaders. The following web shows this relationship.

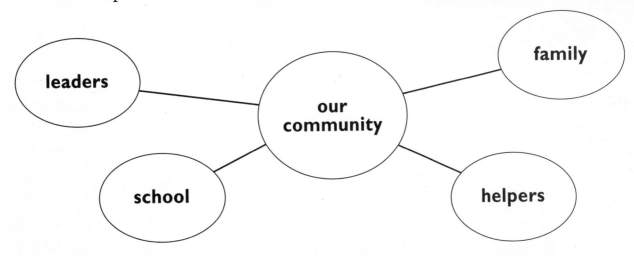

To expand on this relationship, we can ask students to relate community to pollution (science), geography (social studies), population (math), and cultural opportunities (arts). The next web specifies each subcontent and its relationship to the content. It is easy to see the difference in sophistication between the first web and the second web.

Key Teaching Benefits

Use graphic organizers to:

⊕ show and explain relationships between and among content

⊠ make your lessons interactive

⊕ help visual learners to acquire information more easily

⊠ motivate students

⊕ assist students in prewriting techniques

⊠ assess what students know

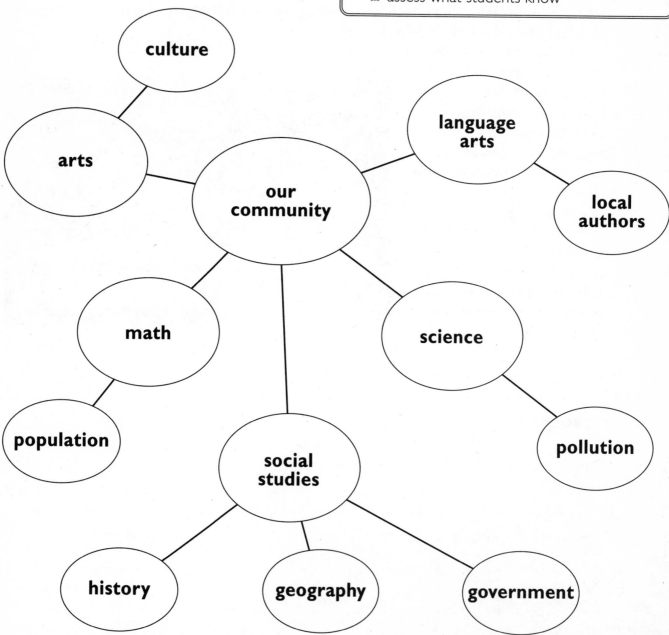

GREAT TEACHING WITH GRAPHIC ORGANIZERS
Scholastic Professional Books, 1998

A visual diagram shows the relationships between information and ideas very effectively. Students are likely to acquire a better understanding of the content of a lesson, because they can see information as connecting parts of a whole rather than isolated facts. Through the use of pictorial outline forms, students can make more abstract comparisons, evaluations, and conclusions. The graphic organizer allows students an active role in the comprehension of information.

Comprehension is also enhanced when students think aloud, discuss, and communicate their thought processes to others. With graphic organizers, students are using a common framework and shared language to easily understand how others in the class have processed their information.

Boosts Thinking Skills

Graphic organizers help students:

- ✦ note patterns
- ✖ better understand the concept of part to whole
- ✦ record relationships
- ✖ find meaning in ideas
- ✦ clarify and organize ideas
- ✖ improve memory
- ✦ comprehend texts
- ✖ recognize and assimilate different points of view
- ✦ represent complex ideas through concise visuals

Connecting With Bloom's Taxonomy

In 1956, prominent educator Benjamin Bloom, along with a group of educational psychologists, classified levels of intellectual behavior that take place in the learning process. Bloom's Taxonomy is one of the most commonly used thinking skills models. The graphic organizers presented in this book are designed to facilitate six levels of thinking Bloom identified: knowledge, comprehension, application, analysis, synthesis, and evaluation.

According to Bloom, the majority of test questions students encounter require only the recall of information. As you will see, graphic organizers offer teachers a variety of techniques for students to apply critical and creative thinking rather than just remembering and regurgitating facts. In order to foster creative and critical thinking in students, educators need to rethink how they teach, and look for methods of instruction and assessment that flex these higher levels of thinking. Graphic organizers provide students with rigorous intellectual workouts and are great tools for encouraging kids to think about their ways of thinking.

One way to help students become aware of their thinking is to have them develop critical and creative thinking skills charts (originally formatted by John Samara of the Curriculum Project and Jim Curry of The Learning Institute). To introduce this idea, explain that *knowledge* is knowing something, *comprehension* is understanding about something, and *applying* is using what one knows and understands. As students grasp these concepts, talk with them about the more challenging levels of thinking. *Analysis* means breaking things up into smaller parts. Students *analyze* when comparing and contrasting. *Synthesis* is another word for creative thinking; some teachers prefer to use the word *creativity*. Talk about imagination and its possibilities. Most students know and understand *evaluation*, but also include decision making and problem solving in this category.

*In Molly's picture, she says she **knows** about houses. She **understands** they can be made out of wood. She says, "I **use** houses to live in." She **compares** wood, brick, and concrete houses. She **creates** brick steps to be used to go in the house. She **judges** her house is the best.*

In the examples on this page, you will see how Molly and Danny, both second graders, show their understanding of Bloom's Taxonomy.

Both Danny and Molly have a basic understanding of the six levels of knowing. They can take a concept and apply it to the taxonomy. They are aware of the type of thinking they are doing. The more they know about their thinking, the better they will become at it.

It is helpful to use graphic organizers to give students exercises that target specific levels of thinking. If students become aware of their thinking processes, they can use each of them more deliberately. It's like playing basketball: If students fool around playing basketball, they may or may not become better at it. If someone coaches them and teaches them how to make a

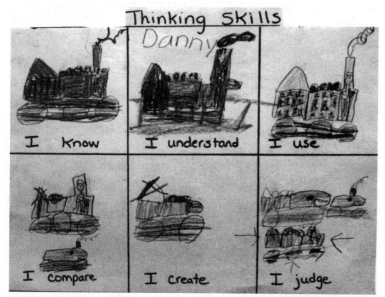

*Danny says he **knows** about trains. He **understands** trains run on tracks. He says they are **used** to carry people. He **compares** types of trains. He **creates** a new type of train, which he **judges** to be the best.*

foul shot, they are aware of how they can become better players. If you want your students to become better at cause/effect relationships, then let them know they are doing cause/effect thinking. At the end of the activity, ask them the specific skills and skill levels they were using. You'll find you will have a lot more critical and creative thinkers at the end of the year. But watch out, you might hear someone say, "We haven't done any creative thinking lessons in a really long time. Can we do some webbing?"

Supporting the Multiple Intelligiences

In his 1983 study *Frames of Mind*, educator Dr. Howard Gardner identified seven multiple intelligences that are often not measured through conventional testing. Graphic organizers can be used in a variety of ways to help develop these multiple intelligences. Here are a few ideas to get you started:

◻ **Verbal/Linguistic:** Use graphic organizers to encourage writing and brainstorming. Students may use organizers to respond to their reading or writing, to generate ideas, to memorize linguistic facts, or to engage in a debate.

◻ **Logical/Mathematical:** Use graphic organizers as a problem-solving tool or as a format for a word problem activity. Graphic organizers can be used as a rough draft to a timeline or to develop a sequence of events (what happened first, second, third, etc.).

◻ **Spatial:** Graphic organizers are perfect for spatially savvy learners. They provide the visual formats these kids need in order to see the whole picture rather than small details. It's natural for spatial learners to organize their ideas into boxes, lists, and the like, so these individuals are not only good at filling in organizers, they're great at designing their own.

◻ **Bodily/Kinesthetic:** Graphic organizers can be used as tools to generate ideas that result in such movement activities as plays. Students can create patterns and designs with objects or pattern blocks and use organizers to record information.

Ready to Start?

Before you jump into using the graphic organizers in this book, there's one question left to consider: *How will you know what organizers to use and when to use them?* To help you figure this out, I've included an Across the Curriculum activity chart at the end of each chapter. To further guide you, think about the following questions when considering using an organizer:

What do I want my students to get out of this lesson?

Is this the best way to reach the objective of the lesson?

Do I have time to do this type of activity?

Do my students know enough information to be successful?

Do my students understand how to use this organizer?

Benefits of Student-Created Organizers

When students create their own graphic organizers:

✦ learning becomes personalized and meaningful

✠ the articulation of knowledge and its relationships becomes essential

✦ creativity is encouraged

✠ self esteem is fostered

✦ motivation is increased

Some of the ready-made organizers presented in this book may not meet your specific needs, so feel free to try modifying some of them by adding lines, shapes, and color. After your students have become familiar with graphic organizers, let them create their own. Actually, some of the graphic organizers in this book are student-generated (by fourth graders). The important thing to remember when designing your own graphic organizer is that it should be pleasing to look at, fun to work with, and provide a meaningful structure in which to record or respond to information.

Tips for Success

Make sure there is a match between the type of organizer and the content. In other words, if teachers are looking for the causes and effects of something, they should use a cause/effect web. If teachers want students to add detail to an idea, they should use an adding detail, or elaboration, graphic. Each graphic organizer is designed to elicit information in a particular way. (Detailed descriptions and examples of specific graphic organizers are provided in Units 1-8.)

✠ **A graphic organizer is not always the best use of time.** Students can answer a direct question much faster than they can plot an answer using a graphic organizer. Each graphic organizer explained in this book discusses the time necessary to ensure success with the strategy. Remember, using graphic organizers is a way to encourage interactive learning and enhance the learning process. Don't use one if it seems to "steal" time from the lesson.

✠ **Use a variety of graphic organizers.** One type of visual does not fit all purposes; therefore, it is necessary to vary the structure of the graphics. Lack of variety can be just as boring as continually presenting information in a lecture format. Be a risk taker: Try different kinds of graphic organizers. You might find yourself opening up entirely new avenues to students who have been struggling in your classroom.

✠ **Use them collaboratively.** Graphic organizers lend themselves to small-group learning. Of course, you must first model how to use the visual so that the class understands how the graphic organizer will function. Filling one out together on an overhead transparency is a dynamic way to demonstrate the organizer's use.

✠ **Tailor the organizers to kids' learning styles.** Some students are quite random in their thought processes and enjoy doing and seeing a web. For other students who are more sequential, a web looks confusing, and they might have

10

difficulty sorting through the brainstormed ideas. Sequential thought processors might be more comfortable with linear material, such as an outline, where the main idea and details are written in a linear format. If you use an outline structure as a follow-up activity to a web, sequential thinkers will be able to make sense of the webbed ideas because the ideas are written in a way that is easy for them to understand.

The following chapters are organized by specific graphic organizers that address particular thinking skills. Each chapter includes a discussion of the thinking strategy, an example of the graphic organizer, step-by-step suggestions on how to introduce it to students, samples of student work, and activities within each content area.

In the Appendix, you'll find lots of reproducible graphic organizers to use. Some are copies of the ones described in the units; others are variations. Your students will find it interesting to try out the different-looking graphics.

Compare and Contrast Organizers

Any time you ask students to identify similarities and differences between things—whether literary characters, species of birds, or types of sports—they are comparing and contrasting. But precisely what thinking skills are involved? Creative thinking is used as students look for more than one similar or different attribute. They use evaluative thinking as they decide how things can be compared. They apply logical reasoning as they define their associations and weed out attributes that don't hold up. In essence, students are breaking up whole things into parts; therefore, the main thinking skill is analysis.

When introducing a compare/contrast organizer, tell students that it allows them to analyze two things. Talk about how compare/contrast thinking is a type of analysis. Encourage them to remember that any time they want to make comparisons or analyze two things, they can use this type of graphic organizer to help them sort through information.

Introducing the Bug Organizer:
A MODEL LESSON

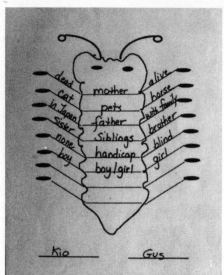

Content of the lesson: *Kio and Gus* by Matthew Lipman

Thinking skill: Compare and contrast/analysis

Graphic organizer: Bug

The bug graphic is designed to compare and contrast two people, places, or things. Common characteristics are written on the bug's body (center lines); the descriptive words or phrases are written on the bug's legs.

I place a transparency of the organizer on the overhead projector and hand out a copy of the bug organizer to each student. I explain to students that this is a graphic organizer used to compare two things, and that I'm going to show them how to use it.

I write the names Kio (the boy in the story) and Gus (the girl in the story) on the lines at the bottom of the bug.

Next, I invite kids to think about these characters, and how they are alike and different. Students offer that Kio's mother is dead, while Gus's mother is alive. So I write *Mother* in the center of the organizer and the words *dead* and *alive* on the respective legs.

I ask, "What is another thing Kio and Gus have in common that we can compare?" "They both have pets," a student offers, and so we write *pets* in the center, and *cat* above Kio's name and *horse* above Gus' name.

"They both had a father, but one was not living with them for the summer," a student suggests. I write *Father* in the center. "So where is Kio's dad?" I ask. The class calls out, "In Japan," and I record this phrase on the chart. On Gus's side I write *with family*.

And so the lesson continues. The students compare siblings, the fact that Gus was blind and Kio could see, and noted that one was a boy and one was a girl. I make an effort to let the students generate the attributes to compare; I want them to get a feel for the difference between attributes

Bug: COMPARE AND CONTRAST

dead — mother — alive
cat — pets — horse
in Japan — father — with family
sister — siblings — brother
none — handicap — blind
boy — boy/girl — girl

Kio _____   Gus _____

The characters Kio and Gus are analyzed on the bug graphic organizer.

GREAT TEACHING WITH GRAPHIC ORGANIZERS
Scholastic Professional Books, 1998

that yield deep insights into the characters, as well as attributes that are factual but don't have much bearing on the story.

At the end of the lesson, I guide students to explain how the characters in the story are alike and different with respect to the attributes they selected. They summarize what they learned. After this model lesson, students are ready to use the graphic organizer on their own.

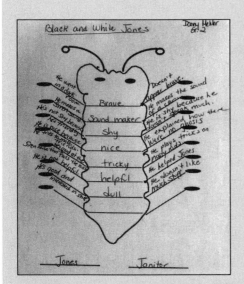

Student in the Spotlight

After the sample lesson, second-grader Danny is asked to compare and contrast two characters from *Black and White Jones* **by Arthur Roth. Here is how Danny, working independently, filled out his bug.**

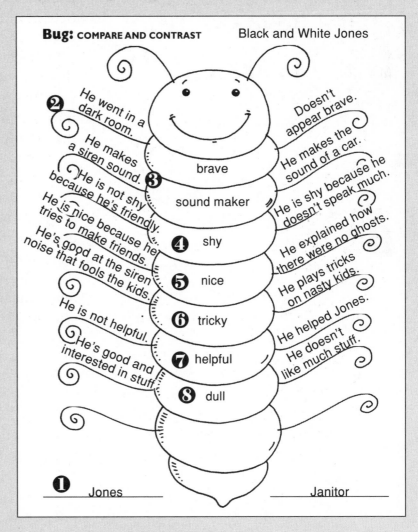

❶ *Danny chooses two characters in the story, Jones and the janitor, and writes their names on the bottom of the graphic.*

❷ *He thinks about the characters. As he writes the characteristic to be compared in the center, he must justify why the character does or does not display this characteristic. Danny thinks Jones is brave because he went in a dark room. He doesn't think the janitor appears brave.*

❸ *Next, Danny examines something rather specific about the characters.*

❹–❽ *He digs deeper, exploring five aspects of the characters' personalities.*

Danny is pleased with his bug. His work on the graphic organizer shows that he remembered many details about the story and understood these characters.

Using the Caterpillar Organizer:
A SAMPLE LESSON

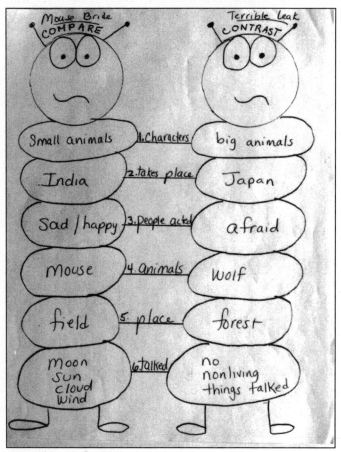

Caterpillar organizer for Mouse Bride *and* The Terrible Leak.

Content of the lesson: *Mouse Bride* by Lucia Turnbull and *The Terrible Leak* by Yashiko Uchida

Thinking skill: Compare and contrast/analysis

Graphic organizer: Caterpillar

The caterpillar, another compare/contrast graphic organizer, was designed by Hannah Fuller, a fourth grader at Mast Landing School in Freeport, Maine. It quickly became a favorite of her classmates.

The caterpillar functions the same way as the bug graphic. It features two caterpillars side by side. The descriptive words and phrases are in the caterpillar's segments with the attributes on lines between them.

The following transcript is from a group that compared two books, *Mouse Bride* and *The Terrible Leak.* You will notice that these students need more practice with the skill of compare and contrast.

Standing at the overhead projector with the caterpillar graphic displayed, I tell the class that they are going to compare and contrast the two stories they've just read. I label the caterpillars *Mouse Bride* and *The Terrible Leak.*

> *"What do you know about the story* Mouse Bride?*" I ask.*
>
> *"It has small animals," a student responds.*
>
> *"Okay, who appears in* The Terrible Leak?*"*
>
> *"Big animals," the class offers.*
>
> *I want my class to think in terms of characters. I ask, "What are the animals called in the story?"*
>
> *"Characters."*
>
> *"Good," I say. I write "character" in the center, and* small animals *and* big animals *in the caterpillars. "What else do you remember about the stories?"*
>
> *"One is in India and one is in Japan," suggests a student.*
>
> *"Yes. India and Japan are where the stories take place. This is known as the setting. What else do you notice about these two stories?"*

GREAT TEACHING WITH GRAPHIC ORGANIZERS
Scholastic Professional Books, 1998

The group seems to have no more ideas to share. They are stuck. To spark discussion, I ask, "How do the people act?" and write people acted *on the third line of the organizer while I wait for a response.*

"In one story the people start off sad and end happy and in the other story, they are afraid," a student says.

"Yes, good," I say, happy students are making richer distinctions between the two stories.

The students point out that one story has a field in it, and the other has a forest in it. They decide to call that a place. *I note that they are recalling what I said earlier about setting.*

The final element kids want to compare is that in one story, the moon, sun, cloud, and wind talk, but in the other story no nonliving thing talks.

I've shared highlights from this lesson to remind you that teaching children to use graphic organizers isn't like following an instant recipe. It often takes time for students to reach higher levels of thinking. I will do another model lesson or two with

Student in the Spotlight

Danny is asked to use the caterpillar organizer to compare two characters in a story. Danny chooses Claire and Robert from *Flood* by Neil R. Selden. He finds the caterpillar works just the same way as the bug and he has no difficulty with the assignment.

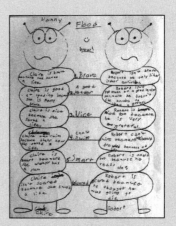

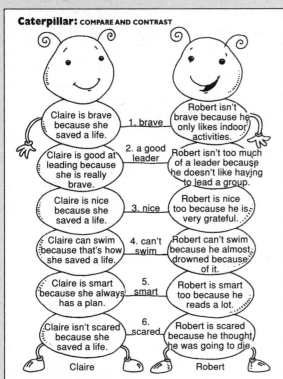

Caterpillar: COMPARE AND CONTRAST

1. *Danny says that Claire is brave because she saves a life, and Robert is not brave because he only likes indoor activities.*

2. *He identifies the characteristic of a good leader and says that Claire is a good leader because she is brave, and Robert is not because he does not like having to lead a group.*

3. *Danny writes that Claire is nice because she saves a life, and Robert is nice too because he is very grateful.*

4. *Danny identifies can't swim as the next characteristic and says that Claire can swim, because that's how she saves a life, and Robert cannot swim, because he almost drowns.*

5. *Danny thinks Claire is smart because she always has a plan, and Robert is smart too because he reads a lot.*

6. *Danny also contrasts the characteristic scared by comparing Claire, who is not scared (because she saves a life) and Robert, who is scared (because he thought he was going to die).*

my students before giving them an organizer to work on independently; my goal is to move my first graders toward more in-depth comparisons.

To conclude the activity, students are asked to share their responses with each other. Because they are using the same organizers, children can easily understand their peers' information. The graphic, then, provides a clear window through which kids see others' thinking processes. It also serves as a quick glimpse of a story they might like to read.

As a finishing touch, the class displays their bugs and caterpillars on the bulletin board.

Some More Tips to Keep in Mind...

- The focus of any compare and contrast activity is analysis. Although it incorporates creative thinking because more than one characteristic is being compared, the emphasis is on critical thinking.
- Make sure students understand the content of the lesson before you give them a compare/contrast organizer. If they do not comprehend or remember the information, they will have a difficult time filling in the graphic. This organizer is best used as a follow-up activity.
- The graphic organizer is easy to use and understand, but sometimes students have difficulty deciding on the characteristics to be compared. If you model a few examples of characteristics, usually students can add a few more on their own. Grouping students can help those who are having difficulty.
- Some students will want to do a rough draft before they fill in their graphic organizer. For example, a student might think about one character first, say Cinderella, and list characteristics about her. Then she would consider a second character, say the fairy godmother, and list her attributes. After brainstorming these lists, the student would enter her ideas on the graphic organizer.
- Students should be able to justify their choices. Ask why they think a character is or is not nice or brave or generous, and so on.
- It is beneficial to have students talk about their responses on the graphic organizer with you, with a peer, or as a class, to reinforce their understanding of the concept.
- Students needn't feel limited by the size of the graphic. Those who have many ideas can use more than one visual.
- Once students are familiar with these graphic organizers, filling one out usually takes 15-20 minutes; however, time can vary quite a bit depending on how difficult the information is that the students are comparing.

Suggested Activities Across the Curriculum

READING WORKSHOP
Use the organizers to compare and contrast:

- fiction and nonfiction
- two characters
- two stories
- types of illustrations in picture books
- the situation in the beginning of the story and at the end of the story
- fairy tales
- heroes and villains in a story

WRITING WORKSHOP
Compare and contrast:

- forms of poetry
- styles of writing
- first drafts and final drafts
- use of descriptive language and "plain" writing
- a student's writing in September and in May

MATH WORKSHOP
Compare and contrast:

- different kinds of triangles (isosceles, right, equilateral, etc.)
- shapes
- calendars
- graphs

SOCIAL STUDIES
Compare and contrast:

- two places of interest
- two celebrations
- two explorers
- two leaders
- two wars

SCIENCE
Compare and contrast:

- mammals and reptiles
- desert and woodland
- kinds of rocks
- planets
- vegetables

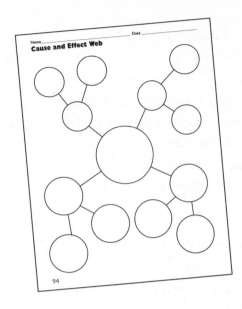

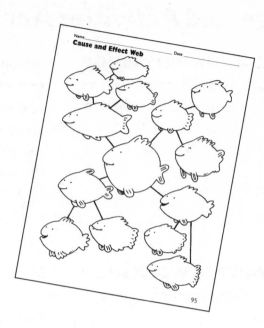

Cause and Effect Web

The purpose of the cause/effect web is to help students analyze the consequences of actions. You can use the web to examine many kinds of topics and concepts. It's a great organizer for looking at the cause and effects surrounding an issue or problem, from dress codes at school to the destruction of the rain forest.

Using these webs taps creative thinking, as students first brainstorm consequences that may not happen but *could* happen; then, they must use evaluative thinking as they decide what actions will cause what results, and rule out some of their brainstormed ideas. The main thinking skill that is emphasized is analysis. As students think of many cause/effect relationships, they must use logical and rational reasoning.

Point out to students that this graphic organizer allows them to analyze a situation or problem using if...then thinking. To help students stay on the cause/effect track and not just brainstorm, use the starter sentence, "If something happens, then what might happen as a result of it?".

This graphic organizer allows students to see that for every action there is a reaction—actions have consequences. Students at my school readily use this organizer to analyze social behaviors. As a class, you could web "What are the effects of acting out with a substitute?". Filling out the web together is a nonthreatening way to look at some touchy issues that arise in the classroom.

An exciting element of the cause/effect web is the way information builds from the main topic (or the cause). Let's say, for instance, that your topic is "Longer School Days." An effect of longer school days might be "Kids Have Less Time to Play." Some effects of kids having less time to play might be "Stores Don't Sell as Many Toys" and "Kids Spend Less Time With Friends." As you can see, the web is building, because each effect then becomes a cause with factors that affect it. As you explore this with your students, they will see how situations and events that seem to be unrelated actually impact each other through a chain of circumstances.

Introducing the Cause and Effect Web
A MODEL LESSON

Content of the lesson: Science/Whales

Thinking skill: Cause and effect/analysis

Graphic organizer: Cause/effect web

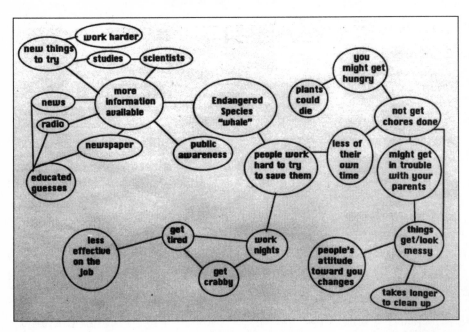

I hand out copies of the cause/effect web to each student and also project it onto a screen with an overhead projector. I tell students we are going to use the graphic to predict possible causes and effects of whales being an endangered species.

I write "endangered species, 'whale'" in the center bubble.

"What are the possible effects of the fact that whales are endangered?" I ask. The students look at me with blank expressions, so I rephrase the question: "If the whales are endangered, then...."

"People work hard to save them," a student suggests.

"Good. Okay, that's an effect of whales being endangered." I trace the line from the center bubble to another bubble, in which I write the student's idea. "Now let's take it and ask ourselves, *What are the consequences, or effects, of people working hard to save them?*"

"They have less of their own time," a student says.

"People may have to work nights, because saving whales is not part of their regular jobs," another child chimes in.

I write these ideas in the bubbles. The students are catching on to cause-and-effect thinking. From there, they brainstorm that the effect of working nights might be that "people might get crabby" because they are overworked and overtired. I write their ideas in the bubbles. I let them offer causes and effects, trying not to lead them in a prescribed direction.

As you can see from the reproduced whale web, some cause and effect chains of thought are more on target than others. For example, the upper left hand side has a strong link between the endangered whale and the effect on public awareness, scientists' careers, coverage of the topic in newspapers, and so forth. The right-hand side illustrates "shakier" conjecture, but that's okay. You want to stretch kids' thinking about a topic. In time, you can get kids to refine their thinking by doing a second draft of the web.

Using the Web to Build Prediction Skills:
A SAMPLE LESSON

Content of the lesson: *Kio and Gus*

Thinking skill: Cause and effect/analysis

Graphic organizer: Cause/effect web

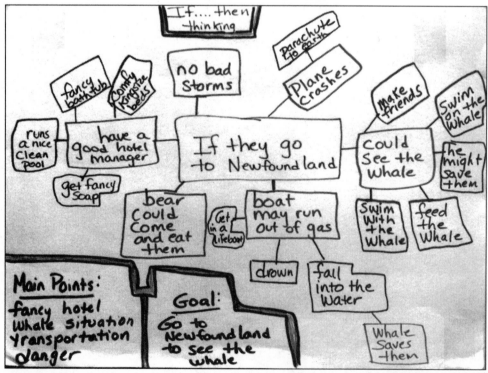

My second graders are in the midst of reading *Kio and Gus*. They're anticipating what it will be like for Grandpa and his family to go to Newfoundland to look for a whale. I draw a web on a big piece of chart paper; together, students brainstorm possible causes and effects of the family going to Newfoundland. Here are highlights of their discussion as they fill in the web:

Second graders came up with this cause/effect web for the book Kio and Gus.

I write the starter phrase, "If they go to Newfoundland...." in the center bubble.

Students suggest possible effects of going to Newfoundland, including:

- they could see the whale
- the boat could run out of gas
- a bear could come and eat them
- they could stay in a hotel with a good manager
- there could be no bad storms
- the plane could crash

Branching out on the web, students decide possible results of seeing the whale might be:

- they make friends
- they could swim on the whale
- the whale might save them
- they could feed the whale

The students consider the possibility of the boat running out of gas. If this happens:

- they might drown
- they might get in a lifeboat
- they might fall in the water

And if they fall in the water, a possible result is:

- the whale could save them

They decide the results of having a good hotel manager could mean:

- you get fancy soap
- there is a nice clean pool
- you might have a fancy bathtub
- there could be comfortable king-size beds

A possible effect of the plane crashing is:

- parachute to earth

My students are pleased with their ideas. They can see that the story can go in many possible directions, and they are anxious to see how their ideas compare with the author's resolution.

Because students' ideas can take off in so many different directions, it is helpful to ask kids to look at their completed webs and determine the main ideas. For example, students decide the main ideas are the fancy hotel, the whale situation, transportation (the boat, the plane), and danger (plane crashing, the bear, boat running out of gas). Next, I ask my students to make an informed prediction about what will happen next in the story, based on their understanding of the book and their responses on the web. After they make their prediction, I ask them to justify their decision.

Fourth Graders Take the Web for a Spin

Toward the end of their persuasive writing unit, a fourth-grade class learns about advertising and propaganda techniques as ways to influence public opinion. Visual as well as verbal messages are analyzed, and the use of animation as an appeal to young audiences is discussed. I talk about how, in the past, animation was primarily used in Saturday morning cartoons or Disney shows. Now, animation can be found in many forms in many places. Students are asked to use the cause/effect web to analyze the effects of increased use of animation. Take a look at how they tackle the assignment.

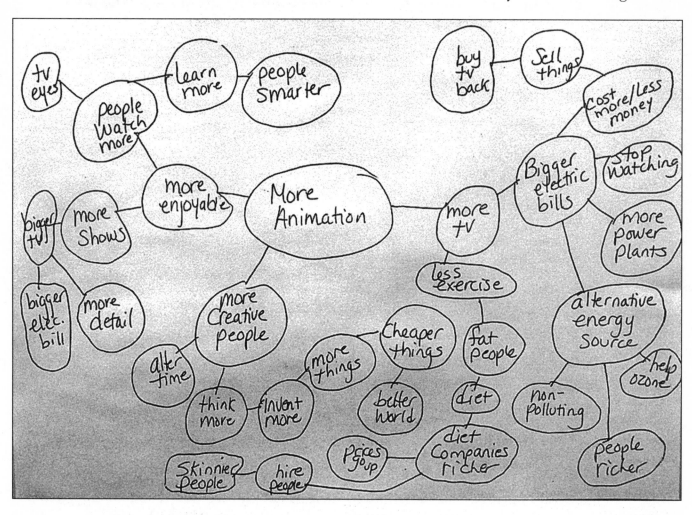

GREAT TEACHING WITH GRAPHIC ORGANIZERS
Scholastic Professional Books, 1998

Some More Tips to Keep in Mind...

✦ The focus of any cause and effect lesson is analysis. It incorporates creative thinking, but the emphasis is on critical thinking.

▨ The lead idea may be presented to students by using *If...then* phrases. Keep repeating *if this...then what.* Some students need to hear it said this way in order for them to make a causal relationship.

✦ After students progress from *if...then,* try asking *what would happen if...* to direct students' thinking. For example, "What would happen if it did not rain or snow for three months?" This leads students to respond by stating effects of the situation.

▨ Encourage students to use the words *might* and *may,* because they are coming up with *possible* effects.

✦ If you are nervous about the activity not addressing the content, record responses but do not build off the ones you think will lead students astray. You can control the flow of the responses. If you allow students to work on their own cause/effect webs, be willing to allow all answers that can be justified even if they go away from the content. Sometimes when students stray from the content, they find themselves connecting back eventually.

▨ Be careful that students do not just look soley at negative effects. If this begins to happen, point it out and ask them to think of some positive effects as well. Sometimes you might even ask them to have as many positive as negative effects. Then they can truly see both sides of an issue.

✦ Bring closure to the activity by pointing out the goals, main points, and/or conclusions that can be made from the ideas generated.

▨ Once the students are familiar with the graphic organizer, the lesson takes about 10-15 minutes to complete.

Suggested Activities Across the Curriculum

READING WORKSHOP
What are the effects of:

- predicting storyline outcomes (What would happen if he doesn't reach his goal?)
- changing the story outcome (What would happen if they had not...)
- character analysis

WRITING WORKSHOP
What are the effects of:

- writing in a genre
- a particular setting for the story (a prewriting activity)
- a particular character for a story (a prewriting activity)
- going to bed later on the weekends or getting a pet (persuasive prewriting activity)

MATH WORKSHOP
What are the effects of:

- no such thing as numbers
- no calculators

SOCIAL STUDIES
What are the effects of:

- invention of the automobile
- homelessness
- watching hours of television a day
- population growth in our community, school, or city
- local issues
- historical issues (i.e., bill of rights)
- a presidential candidate's political views
- no maps
- no post office
- explorers to the New World

SCIENCE
What are the effects of:

- global warming
- weather disasters
- flourishing vegetation in the rainforest
- an oil spill
- naturally caused forest fires

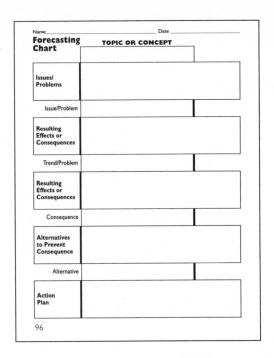

Forecasting Chart

A forecasting chart helps students identify an issue, trend, or problem, analyze it, and develop an action plan. The students are forecasting—addressing a possible future. Creative thinking comes into play with this strategy, because students are offering a variety of ideas as well as developing an action plan. The main thinking skill that is emphasized is analysis.

Point out to students that this graphic organizer allows them to analyze a problem. As students use this graphic organizer to analyze the issue, they must make clear and believable assumptions. They use their imaginations to apply insight to their reasoning. Their ideas must be built logically and be justifiable.

This graphic organizer can be a very empowering tool for students. In some lessons, students can actually carry out the action plan to affect change. For example, my students began with the problem of school behavior and came up with a list of classroom rules they all agreed to follow. Another group of students designed a specific set of safety rules for a field trip based on the broad topic of taking a field trip.

Introducing the Forecasting Chart
A MODEL LESSON

Content of the lesson: Transportation
Thinking skill: Forecasting/analysis
Graphic organizer: Forecasting chart

The forecasting chart builds on the skills exercised by the cause/effect web, but instead of linking an issue with a series of tangents, students use this chart to focus on a single idea. In the following example, I show students how another class began with the topic "transportation" and ended up with an action plan concerning gun control. My students really like seeing what peers have done, and they catch on quickly. Here are the things I point out to them.

Using an overhead projector, I show students a forecasting chart on transportation completed by third graders. I explain that this is a forecasting chart used to analyze a topic or problem.

❶ I point out that the topic is written in the top box.

❷ I show my students that the many issues relating to transportation are recorded in the **Issues/Problems** box.

❸ I point out that the third graders chose one idea they wanted to discuss—safety—from the bigger box and recorded it here.

❹ Next, they identified **many** problems relating to safety and transportation, but recorded only answers built on logical rationale in the **Trends/Problems** box.

❺ Students again focused their ideas by choosing **one** problem to discuss: drive-by shootings. This is their single **Trend/Problem**.

❻ Here they discussed the positive and/or negative effects of this trend and recorded their ideas in this box.

❼ They then chose which effect they wanted to address: increased gun sales.

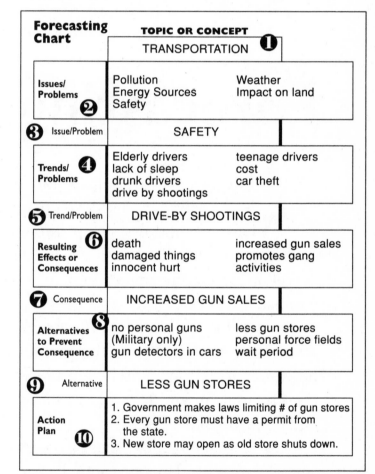

Third graders used this forecasting chart to come up with an action plan concerning gun control.

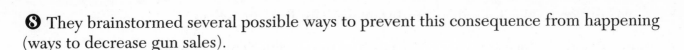

8 They brainstormed several possible ways to prevent this consequence from happening (ways to decrease gun sales).

9 They decided upon one alternative: fewer gun stores.

10 Students presented a three-point action plan designed to limit the number of places to buy guns.

Analyzing A Story Problem With the Forecasting Chart:
A SAMPLE LESSON

Content of lesson: *Kio and Gus*

Thinking skill: Forecasting/analysis

Graphic Organizer: Forecasting chart

My second-grade class is reading *Kio and Gus*. About halfway through the story, I ask my students to analyze Grandpa's problem by filling in the forecasting chart. In case you aren't familiar with the story, Grandpa's problem is: When Grandpa was a boy, he was saved by Leviathan, the whale. Now Grandpa wants to travel to Newfoundland to find Leviathan, to see the whale one more time before he dies.

I act as the recorder. Following are highlights of their discussion:

1. Students identify the **topic of concern**: Grandpa and Leviathan.

2. Students identify two **Issues/Problems**: how tough it will be to leave the

Forecasting Chart	TOPIC OR CONCEPT
	Grandpa and Leviathan
Issues/ Problems	how tough it will be to leave the farm and go to Newfoundland; and they may not find the whale
Issue/Problem	they may not find the whale
Trends/ Problems	Grandpa may be disappointed; the whale could have died; the boat may break; and they could drown trying to find the whale
Trend/Problem	Grandpa's disappointment
Resulting Effects or Consequences	Grandpa will be sad for a long time; he might think the whale died; he might not talk to anyone (because he becomes depressed); and he might get angry when they talk about the whale.
Consequence	Grandpa being sad for a long time
Alternatives to Prevent Consequence	Give him a party; give him a mug with a picture of a whale on it; go to an aquarium to visit a different whale; talk to him about the whale; or get him a pet whale.
Alternative	give him a mug with a picture of a whale on it
Action Plan	a five-point Action Plan

farm and go to Newfoundland; and they may not find the whale.

3. They decide to focus on "they may not find the whale." This becomes the **Issue/Problem**.

4. The **Trends/Problems** surrounding not finding the whale include: Grandpa may be disappointed; the whale could have died; the boat may break; and they could drown trying to find the whale.

5. The **Trend/Problem** they focus on is Grandpa's disappointment.

6. The **Resulting Effects or Consequences** could be: Grandpa will be sad for a long time; he might think the whale died; he might not talk to anyone (because he becomes depressed); and he might get angry when they talk about the whale.

7. Students choose to focus on the **Consequence** of Grandpa being sad for a long time.

8. Students come up with **Alternatives to Prevent This Consequence**: Give him a party; give him a mug with a picture of a whale on it; go to an aquarium to visit a different whale; talk to him about the whale; or get him a pet whale.

9. After much discussion, the group decides the best **Alternative** is to give him a mug with a picture of a whale on it.

10. The second graders come up with a five-point **Action Plan** to make Grandpa happy. The steps to their plan include:

   ⊠ they make sure they have some money;

   ⊠ they will call around and see if a store has a mug with a picture of a whale on it;

   ⊠ if not, they will get a picture of a whale and bring it to a store that will make a mug with the picture on it;

   ⊠ they will buy the mug;

   ⊠ they will give it to Grandpa.

   Students are satisfied with their plan. They have an alternative idea in mind just in case Grandpa does not find the whale in the story. Of course, in the end, Grandpa does get to see the whale one last time; however, students think their ending for the story would have been just fine too. With this graphic organizer, second graders need to be shown more than one example before they are ready to venture forward without direct teacher guidance.

Students Chart a Book Independently

Content of the lesson: *Effie Whittlesy* by George Ade

Thinking skill: Forecasting/analysis

Graphic organizer: Forecasting chart

In the story *Effie Whittlesy*, Effie is a servant who calls her employer, Mr. Wallace, by his first name, Ed. Mr. Wallace finds this behavior unacceptable and fires Effie. Three fourth grade students who read the story find this an injustice and decide to use the forecasting chart to analyze the situation. Here are the steps of their process:

❶ Students identify the main character, Effie Whittlesy, as the topic.

❷ They identify three problems or thoughts about Effie.

❸ They identify one of Effie's problems: she calls her employer by his first name.

❹ They discuss related problems based on this situation.

❺ They choose to focus on the problem of Effie being forced to leave.

❻ They identify the effects of Effie leaving.

❼ Students identify Effie's problem: she no longer has a job.

❽ They discuss how Effie's problem could have been prevented so that she would still have a job.

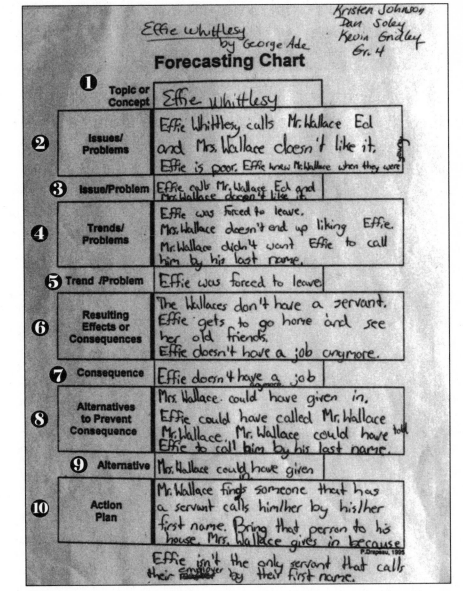

❾ Students decide Mr. Wallace is being unreasonable and decide to have him give in and accept Effie calling him Ed.

❿ The way students decide to convince Mr. Wallace to do this is:

⊠ have him find someone who has a servant who calls him/her by his/her first name;

☒ bring the person to Mr. Wallace's house;

☒ have Mr. Wallace give in because he finds out Effie isn't the only servant who calls his/her employer by his/her first name.

The fourth grade students are enthusiastic about their ending. They think it is much better than the actual story ending.

With fourth graders and on up to higher grade levels, this graphic organizer can be quickly shown, explained, and used. Each box is clearly labeled and students seem to be able to work fairly quickly in small groups or independently to arrive at an action plan.

Some More Tips to Keep in Mind...

✦ The focus of this strategy is analysis. As such, it includes creative thinking but especially emphasizes critical thinking.

☒ The graphic organizer may be used to address any topic, issue, problem, or concern.

✦ The teacher may need to model more than one or two samples lessons, especially with young students.

☒ Let students work together before expecting individuals to complete a forecasting chart on his/her own.

✦ The teacher may ask a student to justify or clarify a response if it does not seem logical.

☒ The graphic organizer has many steps but may be simplified by removing steps if appropriate to the content of the lesson or the ability of the students.

✦ *Do not eliminate the action plan.* It is the piece that empowers students and allows them to see how they have the potential to affect change.

☒ Make sure students understand the last step is a plan and not a list of do's and don'ts.

✦ Once students are familiar with this graphic organizer, the lesson takes about 20-30 minutes to complete.

Student in the Spotlight

Midway through a unit on inventions, my fourth graders are asked to come up with an idea for an invention. Once they have the idea, they are asked to analyze it by using the forecasting chart. Here is how Jeff Smith tackled the challenge:

1. Jeff brainstorms issues/problems/concerns regarding his invention: a pen-holding hat.

2. He identifies possible problems of his pen-holding hat: holding only two pens; trouble sewing the holder on the hat; and looking ridiculous.

3. He decides to focus on the idea that the hat would only hold two pens. (Note: This is a fairly easy problem to solve.)

4. The effects of only holding two pens might be that they both run out of ink and you might want to use a marker or pencil, in which case your hat would not help you.

5. The student decides to focus on the problem of limiting what you can use.

6. In order not to limit the use of the hat to pen holding, the alternatives are to sew on more things, make sure the material won't stretch so that the writing tools won't fall out of their holders, and maybe make the loops adjustable.

7. This student decides to sew on more things.

8. His action plan starts out with finding material, placing writing things in a place that won't be annoying, sewing on the loops, and testing it out.

Jeff Smith
Grade 4

Forecasting Chart

Topic or Concept	invention
Issues/ Problems	improving pen holding hat make new invention research my invention selling my invention
Issue/Problem	Pen holding hat
Trends/ Problems	holds only 2 pens may not be able to sew the holder on the hat may look ridiculous
Trend /Problem	Holds only 2 pens
Resulting Effects or Consequences	Pens run out of ink may want to use a maker or pencil
Consequence	Limits what you can use
Alternatives to Prevent Consequence	Sew on more things make sure material won't stretch maybe make loops adjustable
Alternative	Sew on more things
Action Plan	1. Find more material 2. place pens in a place that won't be annoying. 3. Sew on the loops 4. test it out.

P. Drapeau, 1995

Scholastic Professional Books, 1998

Suggested Activities Across the Curriculum

READING WORKSHOP
Analyze problems relating to:

- a situation in a story
- characters in a story
- what would happen if the story took place in our town
- a book project

WRITING WORKSHOP
Analyze problems relating to:

- a character you develop
- a situation between two characters you develop
- finding time to write and revise
- handwriting a story

MATH WORKSHOP
Analyze problems relating to:

- not being able to use a calculator in math
- what would happen if the U.S. converted to the metric system
- the population figures in your state, and forecast a possible problem
- preparing for a math meet

SOCIAL STUDIES
Analyze problems relating to:

- safety rules in our community
- discrimination
- immigration to the U.S.
- airline industry
- freedom of speech

SCIENCE
Analyze problems relating to:

- water pollution
- rainforest
- recycling
- strip mining (rocks and minerals unit)
- colonization in space
- weather disasters

GREAT TEACHING WITH GRAPHIC ORGANIZERS
Scholastic Professional Books, 1998

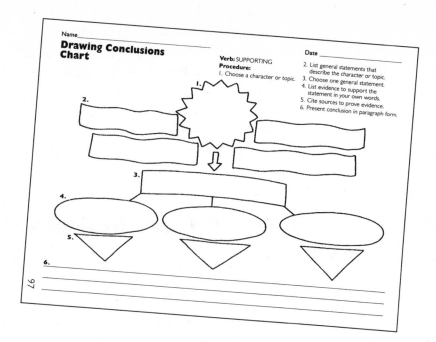

Drawing Conclusions Chart

The drawing conclusions chart is designed to help students analyze and verify information through supportive statements and then form conclusions based on evidence. Using the chart focuses students' attention on high-level critical thinking. Though a very structured analytical process, this strategy does involve creativity, as students brainstorm and entertain many statements about a situation before making a conclusion. The main thinking skill that is emphasized is evaluation.

I've found that many students are unaware of how the drawing-conclusions process actually works, so this organizer is a real asset. As they fill it out, students can see each step of the process of drawing conclusions. And for teachers, the graphic helps them to see where students' thinking breaks down. A teacher can look at the visual and direct the lesson to a specific subskill if students are stuck. When students draw inaccurate or unsubstantiated conclusions, they can refer to the graphic to see where they made their mistakes.

The beauty of this graphic is that it calls upon many skills. Students learn how to skim for information as they look to support their statements. They summarize information and draw conclusions when they make their generalizations. At first glance, it may look complex for young learners; however, the process is so clearly defined that any age child can use this graphic and accomplish the objective of drawing a conclusion.

This graphic organizer was designed by Deborah Gotts, from Mahoney Middle School in South Portland, Maine, and Anne Rodier, from Sea Road School in Kennebunk, Maine. The following introductory lesson was also developed by Deborah and Anne.

Introducing the Drawing Conclusions Chart:
A MODEL LESSON

Content of the lesson: *Tom Sawyer* by Mark Twain

Thinking skill: Drawing conclusions/evaluation

Graphic organizer: Drawing conclusions chart

The drawing conclusions chart is an excellent tool for character analysis. If your students have read *Tom Sawyer*, use the following lesson—just photocopy and enlarge the organizer on this page. If your students haven't read the book, use the lesson to help develop your own model based on a novel your students have read recently.

I project the completed Tom Sawyer chart onto a screen. I explain to students that this graphic organizer is designed to help them draw conclusions, and that I'm showing them how other students filled it out so they will know how it works.

1. I point out that the topic, Tom Sawyer (the main character), is placed in the sun shape at the top.

2. "Four general statements were made about Tom Sawyer," I say, pointing to: *Tom has a curious nature; Tom is in love with Becky; Tom is a clever boy; and Tom is mischievous.*

3. Next, the students chose one of those statements from which to draw conclusions. In this example, "Tom is a clever boy" is selected.

4. Here, students provided three ideas to back up the statement "Tom is a clever boy": *Tom gets others to do his work; Tom seems to come out of trouble smelling like a rose; and Tom is very creative with a good imagination.*

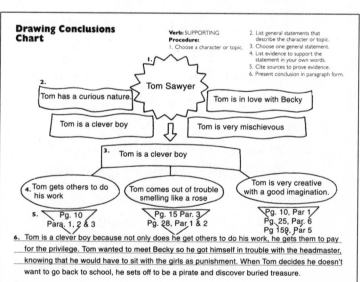

5. I tell the class, "Notice that the students cited page numbers and paragraphs from the

book to justify each idea." It's vital to underscore that each idea must be justified.

6. The final step is to draw conclusions about Tom Sawyer based on the information presented. This is an important step because the generalizations are not solely the readers' opinions. Remember: All opinions and statements are supported by factual references. Conclusions are made about Tom Sawyer based on the information recorded on the graphic organizer.

Because there are many steps to the drawing conclusions chart, the procedure is printed in the upper left hand corner, so that students can refer to it if they do not remember what to do next. The verb *supporting* is noted, because the emphasis on drawing conclusions is based on supporting information. It is important for students to keep this in mind.

Second Graders' Surprising Tangents:
A SAMPLE LESSON

Content of the lesson: *Town Mouse and Country Mouse* by Jan Brett

Thinking skill: Drawing conclusions/evaluation

Graphic organizer: Drawing conclusions chart

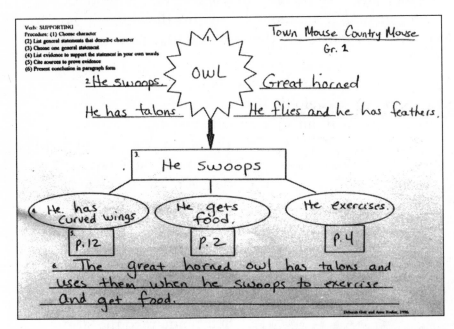

After explaining how the chart works, I ask a small reading group to try one. I have just read *Town Mouse and Country Mouse* to the students. At the end of the story, I ask the group to choose a character about which to draw conclusions. I expect students to choose either the town mouse or the country mouse, and I'm surprised when they opt for the owl. Now the owl has very little to do with the story, and I am hesitant to use this character; however, I decide to honor the students' choice and see what happens. Since this is the first time the students have tried using this graphic organizer, I decide to act as the recorder, and the students work through the process as a group.

I write the word "owl" in the sun shape.

"What do you know about the owl in the story?" I ask.

"He swoops," a student offers.

Other students chime in: "He has talons"; "he is a great horned owl"; and "he flies and has feathers." I record their ideas.

GREAT TEACHING WITH GRAPHIC ORGANIZERS
Scholastic Professional Books, 1998

37

"Great," I say. "Now, choose one idea you would like to look at closely." The students choose
He swoops.

"Okay, based on the story, tell me how you know the owl swoops." The students respond: He
has curved wings (so he can swoop); he gets food (why he needs to swoop); and he exercises
(why he swoops).

I then ask students to defend their ideas by citing examples from the story. I am concerned
because I feel the students made up some of the answers, and they may not find support for
their ideas in the story. Because Town Mouse and Country Mouse is a picture book, students
are allowed to use illustrations as well as text to support their ideas.

Much to my surprise, students are able to support each claim about the owl with either text
or pictures. The pages in the story are not numbered, so the students count the pages and note
the page number in the box to show where they find support for their ideas.

Now the hard part—to draw conclusions about the owl based on the facts. My students com-
bine their ideas to form a statement. They say, "The great horned owl has talons and uses them
when he swoops to exercise and get food."

I share this lesson with you to underscore the importance of allowing students to
pursue their ideas. As teachers, it's always tempting to do lots of backseat driving in
our quest to have lessons turn out well. Here, despite working with a minor character, students did all the "right thinking" I wanted them to do—they learned how to
skim for information to support their ideas, and they learned that they need to substantiate their ideas.

A New Twist on Book Reports

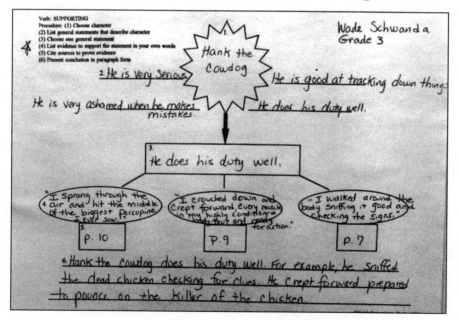

Burnt out from assigning the
traditional book report? Use
one of these organizers
instead! Even though the
focus is more specific than a
book report, it nonetheless
invites the student to show
what he knows about the
story. Third grader Wade
Schwanda read the story
Hank the Cowdog and then
reported on the book. He successfully leads us to believe
that Hank is one smart dog!

To extend this literature
response activity, you may
wish to ask kids to illustrate their conclusions; to design a diorama that demonstrates
their conclusions; or to present their conclusions to the class by acting out the specific examples cited in the story.

GREAT TEACHING WITH GRAPHIC ORGANIZERS
Scholastic Professional Books, 1998

Student in the Spotlight

Third-grader Clark Sleeth is asked to read a biography and draw conclusions about the person. He chooses Laura Ingalls. In the graphic below, I've highlighted the steps of the process and the skills Clark used as he proceeded. As you can see, this type of organizer is very effective in training students to look back at the text to find concrete support for their ideas. Clark cites page numbers, uses direct quotes, and paraphrases as he builds his case.

Content of the lesson: Biography

Thinking skill: Drawing conclusions/evaluation

Graphic organizer: Drawing conclusions chart

2. Clark shows a good understanding of Laura's character: loves her family; likes to hear stories; likes to have fun; and likes cooking.

3. He chooses to concentrate on the general statement Laura likes to cook.

4. He supports his choice by saying she: likes butchering time; likes churning butter; and likes maple syrup.

5. Clark finds evidence in the story to support the three ideas and lists page numbers to indicate where he found his evidence.

6. Clark is able to present a conclusion. "Laura Ingalls likes to cook. At butchering time, she likes to make a balloon out of the pig's tail. The best part of churning was watching the butter fall out of the butter mold. At maple syrup time, she likes to make maple syrup candies. Of all the days of the week, she liked cooking days best of all."

Clark shows that he clearly understands the information he read about Laura Ingalls. He is able to identify interesting facts about her life, support his ideas from examples in the story, and draw conclusions about her. His teacher can see that he is a good analytical thinker, can skim for information, and can synthesize facts.

Some More Tips to Keep in Mind...

✦ This activity encourages students to analyze and evaluate. Students must call upon their logical thinking skills to synthesize the information when they make conclusions.

✖ Students must have a way to substantiate their ideas. They need direct access to information, and they must cite sources. Through the specific steps incorporated in the process, students see that summarizing information and justifying ideas are means to making reliable conclusions.

✦ This activity is always a follow-up activity to an assignment.

✖ Remind students that the steps are laid out for them on the upper left hand corner of the organizer. Each step is clearly defined and will remind them of what to do next.

✦ Sometimes a topic is very limited and may cause students to come up with few reasons to substantiate their ideas. If students cannot fill in all the spaces, encourage them to fill in as many ideas as possible.

✖ If students need more spaces than what is on the paper, they can use two papers for one topic. Generally students will not want to use two papers and manipulate that many ideas; however, there are some students who will appreciate more space for information.

✦ Sometimes students have trouble moving from choosing a statement about their ideas to listing the evidence in their own words to support their statements. To move them to this next step use the question, "Why do you think this?"

✖ Sometimes students have trouble making the conclusion. They often directly restate the ideas specified on the paper. They combine the ideas exactly as they are written above. It is okay for students to do this at first. They need lots of modeling before they learn how to synthesize information by rewording it.

✦ This activity takes about 20-30 minutes to complete. The time frame can vary depending on the complexity of the information.

GREAT TEACHING WITH GRAPHIC ORGANIZERS
Scholastic Professional Books, 1998

Suggested Activities Across the Curriculum

READING WORKSHOP
Draw conclusions about:
+ a character
+ a place
+ why you like (don't like) a book
+ a surprise ending
+ biography

WRITING WORKSHOP
Draw conclusions about:
+ a writing piece
+ an advertising technique
+ why you think a writing piece is good (not good)

MATH WORKSHOP
Draw conclusions about:
+ a banking system
+ the use of Roman numerals
+ fractions
+ geometric shapes

SOCIAL STUDIES
Draw conclusions about:
+ an explorer
+ a place
+ homelessness
+ poverty
+ a presidential point of view
+ the Civil War
+ pros/cons of prisons

SCIENCE
Draw conclusions about:
+ space travel
+ environmental clean-up efforts
+ care of pets
+ birds' homes
+ protection of wild animals
+ the rainforest

Creative Thinking Chart

Creative thinking—we know it when we see it or hear it, but what exactly does it entail? Author and educator E. Paul Torrance teased apart creativity into four elements—fluency, flexibility, originality, and elaboration. Creative thinking charts are designed to flex these four skills.

Working with these charts is essentially a two-part activity. First, students learn to be fluent in their thinking. They're given a topic and asked to come up with ideas relating to it as swiftly as they can. They record their brainstorms on the organizer. Then, students take their lists and categorize them. By placing ideas in categories, students learn to synthesize their ideas. When they're done, they can check to see how diverse their ideas are. If they have twenty ideas that all fall into two categories, they—and you—will know they need to become more flexible in their thinking. If their brainstorms span several domains, they're thinking creatively about the topic!

In this unit examples of two different types of graphic organizers are used to elicit creative thinking. They are the turtle and the creative thinking chart. The pot of gold and cream soda cafe organizers, on pages 99 and 101, work in a similar manner. Let's take a look at the examples.

Introducing the Turtle:
A MODEL LESSON

Content of the lesson: Science/Rocks
Thinking skill: Creative thinking/synthesis
Graphic organizer: Turtle

When I introduce a creative-thinking activity I often say to students, "Think of many different kinds of...." This signals to them to let their imaginations take flight. You'll find that students get the hang of this organizer fast; one introductory lesson usually does the trick.

When using the turtle organizer, students record their ideas on the turtle's shell. After coming

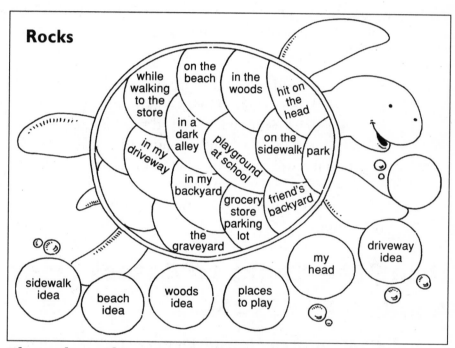

The turtle graphic was originally designed by Liz Geredien, a fourth grader at Mast Landing School in Freeport, Maine and has been slightly modified.

up with numerous ideas, students categorize their lists and place their categories in the bubbles around the turtle.

1. I hand out or project on an overhead a copy of the turtle graphic, and explain to students that this type of graphic organizer is used to help them brainstorm and then categorize their ideas.

2. I tell students that the class that completed this organizer had been studying rocks. One day the teacher brought in rocks she had collected. The teacher asked her students to think of many, different places she could have found the rocks.

3. I say, "The students had five minutes to brainstorm places while their teacher recorded their ideas," and I point to the text inside the shell. "All these ideas show that the class

did a good job coming up with many ideas in a limited time frame."

4. I tell my students that the next step is to look at how different the ideas are. I point to the bubbles around the turtle, and tell students that the words represent the categories into which the kids' sorted their ideas. For example, they decided to label "while walking to the store" and "the sidewalk" responses as a sidewalk category. The only beach idea is "on the beach." "In the woods" and "the graveyard" fit into a woods category. They put "in my backyard," "the park," and "my friend's backyard" in the play category. "Hit on the head" is the only head idea. "In my driveway," "in a dark alley," and "in the grocery store parking lot" are considered driveway ideas.

5. I remark that the class came up with 13 ideas. The 13 ideas fit into six different categories—pretty good proof of flexible thinking.

6. I wrap up the lesson by pointing out that the organizer taps two kinds of creative thinking skills: fluent and flexible thinking. Together, we discuss the differences between the two kinds of thinking.

Remind students that there is no right or wrong category for an idea as long as they can defend their choices. If students argue over which category an idea fits into, ask the student who offered the idea to decide. Chances are the student had something in mind when he made the suggestion. For example, students might argue that a watch can be placed in the *useful* category or the *decorative* category, but if the student who suggested *watch* was thinking of it as stylish jewelry, then he would want it in the decorative category. An idea can also be placed in more than one category.

Using the Chart to Assess Prior Knowledge:
A SAMPLE LESSON

Content of the lesson: Mystery stories
Thinking skill: Creative thinking/synthesis
Graphic organizer: Turtle

At Mast Landing School, fourth graders in a reading group have just been introduced to a unit on mystery stories. I use the turtle chart as a creative-thinking activity to assess what students already know about this literary genre. The students are asked to think as a group about many, different words to describe mystery stories. A student in the group records their ideas on the graphic organizer.

1. I hand out a copy of the turtle graphic and remind the group that the purpose of brainstorming is to come up with as many words as possible that fit the situation.

2. The recorder writes *mysteries* on the bottom of the paper.

3. Students brainstorm words relating to mystery stories. The words are written in a random order as they come to mind.

44

4. Next, students categorize their ideas and list them in each bubble. The group decides to put the word "scary" into the category *feelings*. "Murder," "stolen," "chase," and "confession" are things that *happen*. A "problem solver," "a suspect," "a witness," and "a detective" are *people*. A "problem" is called a *problem*. "Evidence," "a magnifying glass," "a motive," and "clues" are things that are *used*. "Dangerous" and "risk" are *feelings*. A "lie detector" and a "code" are *communication forms*.

This group did an admirable job and conveyed to me that they knew a good deal about the mystery genre. They came to a consensus with their ideas and used many vocabulary words appropriate to mystery stories. As a follow-up activity, they might illustrate one of their ideas or restructure their ideas in a linear fashion by prioritizing what is most important to least important or what would happen first, second, third, etc. Students can complete these activities individually or in their small groups.

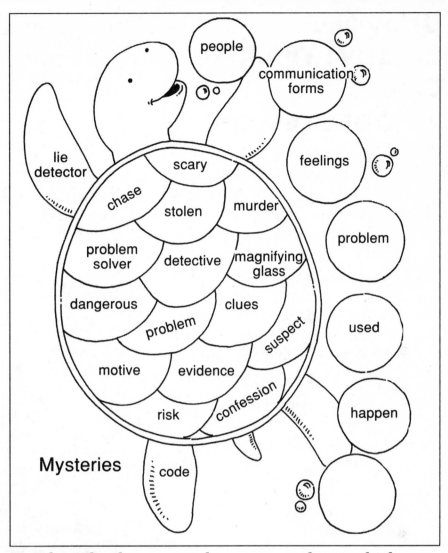

Fourth graders brainstormed mysteries on their turtle chart.

Using the Creative Thinking Chart:
A MODEL LESSON

Sequential thinkers prefer the linear format of the creative thinking chart. In the following example, students in my third-grade class are studying the circus. About midway through the unit, I ask students to consider what might be a good gift to give a circus performer. They define a good gift as something a person might need or enjoy having.

- The students respond to the question "What are the many, different gifts you could give a circus performer?"

- I record the students' answers

- After much discussion, the students categorize their ideas. This group comes up with nine categories.

- They use two papers to accommodate the extra ideas and categories.

The creative thinking chart was originally designed by Nick Heinz, a fourth grader at Mast Landing School in Freeport, Maine. The chart has been slightly modified.

What are the many gifts you could give a circus performer?

- ☑ banners
- ☑ Colored teeth
- ☑ toys
- ☑ popcorn
- ☑ make-up
- ☑ whip
- ☑ certificate to a costume store
- ☑ new animal
- ☑ pictures of their family
- ☑ recipes for food

decoration	Cosmetics	entertainment
banners pictures of their family	Colored teeth make-up fake hair fake fingernails	gags juggling balls tightrope

food	tools	money
popcorn recipes for food	toys whip microphone	Certificate to a costume store

- ☑ Costume
- ☑ gags
- ☑ fake fingernails
- ☑ juggling balls
- ☑ tightrope
- ☑ fake hair
- ☑ television
- ☑ microphone
- ☐
- ☐

clothes	animals	job related
costume	new animal	television

Third Graders Imagine The Westward Movement

My third grade class is studying the Westward Movement. About halfway through the unit, as students learn about the trail drives in the 1850s, I want to see what my students have learned about the westward movement so far. I put a creative thinking chart on the overhead projector and tell my class to pretend they are on the trail drive. Imagine, I say, you find something on the trail. What might that be? I remind the students that even though they are brainstorming, the responses still must be accurate for the 1850s—Howard Johnson's restaurants or a pair of sneakers are not likely! Here is how my students organized their ideas on the chart.

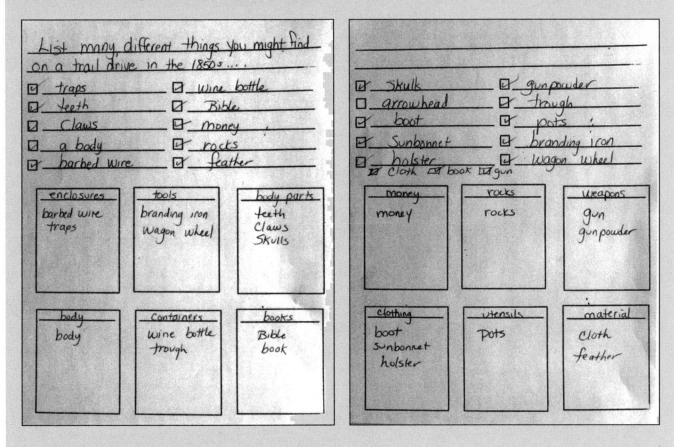

To conclude the activity, students use their ideas to generate a creative writing story. Each story must include at least five of the items from the list. The story does not have to do with finding something on a trail drive, but the trail must be the setting, and the story must take place in 1850.

One class used their creative thinking exercise to make an illustrated booklet about the circus.

Some More Tips to Keep in Mind...

✦ Creative thinking is meant to be open-ended with the possibility of many answers.

✖ Student responses should reflect an understanding of the content of the lesson. On the other hand, you don't want straight recall of facts; ideally, students will use their knowledge to generate informed, imaginative ideas. For example, students may not have known from research that skulls lay along the trail, but it's a reasonable, creative idea to infer.

✦ If your objective is to have students come up with lots of ideas, just ask students to brainstorm, and skip the categorizing phase of the lesson. It would take too long to categorize so many ideas, and students would get frustrated.

✖ Some students have difficulty writing their ideas in the space on the turtle's back; the same is true of the lines on the thinking-skills chart. While it's good practice for kids to have to distill their ideas into a few words

that will fit into the graphic, feel free to modify the organizer to fit your students' needs.

✦ Don't hesitate to let students come up with obscure categories that can accommodate only one idea. They will want to make lots of categories once they figure out that flexibility is encouraged. Let them go ahead and do this.

✖ Remember, if there is any debate over where an idea fits, the judgment call should be made by the person who originated the idea. That person decides if it fits in one or more categories. If no one remembers who stated the idea, the group can decide.

✦ Generally, let students brainstorm for about 5 minutes. This gives them time to think beyond the common responses but not too much time to generate a huge list of ideas. The whole activity, brainstorming and categorizing, takes about 15 minutes.

Suggested Activities Across the Curriculum

READING WORKSHOP
Think of the many, different:

- ways to solve the problem in the story
- titles for the story
- characters in literature
- ways to improve a character in the story
- ways to illustrate a story
- ways to make a story book

WRITING WORKSHOP
Think of the many, different:

- ways to convince people about something you want
- research topics you want to write about
- time periods you could write about
- ways you could get your writing piece published
- ways you could describe an object

MATH WORKSHOP
Think of the many, different:

- forms of money
- ways to spend one million dollars
- ways to demonstrate fractions
- ways fractions are used in real life
- ways we use math in real life
- uses for a calculator
- ways to make the math team

SOCIAL STUDIES
Think of the many, different:

- ways Christopher Columbus could be considered a villain or a hero
- things community helpers do

SCIENCE
Think of the many, different:

- things to do in the snow (rain, cold)
- ways to make a vehicle out of junk
- animal habitats
- tools to measure rain
- ways to provide health services
- ways a pulley can be used

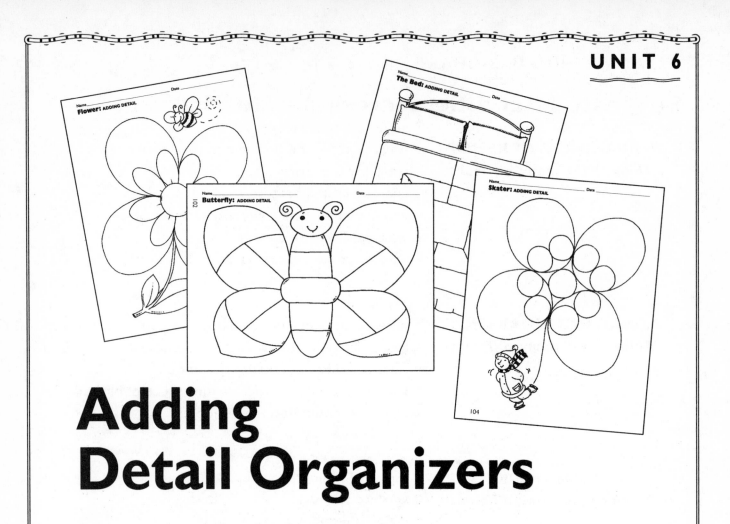

Adding Detail Organizers

You know the scene: After a good half hour of writing time, a few students have penned one idea or sentence—and say they are finished. You ask them to go back and add more detail...and lo and behold, they manage to write one more idea or sentence which is just "more of the same" and doesn't really add the detail you'd like to see.

As long as there are students and stars in the sky, it's going to be a challenge to teach children to elaborate in their writing. It's a fairly abstract concept for children to understand. That said, adding detail organizers will make this an easier skill to teach.

Before using these organizers with my students, I model what I mean by adding detail. I give them a general sentence: "Our eyes are amazing instruments that let us see many things." After a pause, I ask, "That sounds kind of flat, right?" Then I restate it, adding vivid details: "Our eyes are amazing instruments. We use them to see such things as a bright red apple, the little tiny veins in each leaf, or the sunlight sparkling on the ocean." Students easily identify which sentence is more detailed and interesting.

With the butterfly adding detail graphic, students have a visual structure that leads them, step by step, to combine two ideas into one creative and detailed sentence. The format enables them to use both knowledge and their imaginations to make ideas more expressive.

This graphic hones skills relating to creative thinking and synthesis. As with many graphic organizers, it's a great motivator. Students enjoy using this tool. Often, I have students ask to take the organizer home for fun!

Introducing the Butterfly Graphic: A MODEL LESSON

Content of the lesson: Cinderella

Thinking skill: Adding detail/synthesis

Graphic organizer: Butterfly

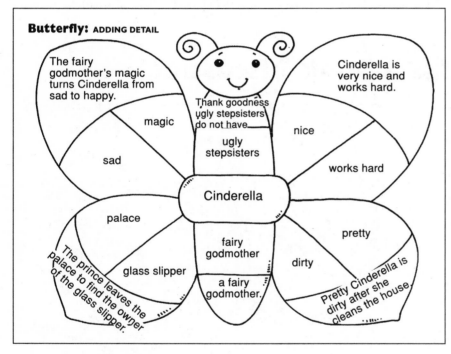

Butterfly: ADDING DETAIL

The fairy godmother's magic turns Cinderella from sad to happy.

magic

sad

Thank goodness ugly stepsisters do not have.

ugly stepsisters

Cinderella

palace

fairy godmother

glass slipper

a fairy godmother.

The prince leaves the palace to find the owner of the glass slipper.

nice

works hard

pretty

dirty

Cinderella is very nice and works hard.

Pretty Cinderella is dirty after she cleans the house.

The first part of using the butterfly graphic involves brainstorming. Students are given a topic and are asked to come up with words that describe it. Students then have to use those words, in specified combinations, to create a descriptive sentence. The following lesson on Cinderella can easily be recreated in your classroom.

The butterfly design was modified by Betsy Webb, a computer teacher at Thorton Academy. The original design was formatted by Thelma Epley in Models of Thinking.

1. Photocopy the butterfly format, and make an overhead transparency of it. Explain that this type of organizer is used to add detail to an idea or concept.

2. Place the name Cinderella in the center box. Explain to students that a character, subject, main idea, topic, or problem may be placed in the center rectangle.

3. Invite students to come up with words that describe Cinderella. Record their ideas in the spaces around the center box. Any word associated with Cinderella is acceptable. Place the first idea in the top center space and place the rest of the words in the spaces going in a clockwise direction.

4. Look at the words in the two spaces in the upper left corner (*sad* and *magic*). Create a strong, descriptive sentence using these two words. Write the sentence in the circle (part of the butterfly's wing) that connects the two spaces. The actual word from the center space (Cinderella) does not have to be restated in the sentence; however, the newly formed sentence does have to relate to the story: **The fairy godmother's *magic* turns Cinderella from *sad* to *happy***. Repeat the process for each corner of the wings.

5. Take the two ideas from the two center spaces and combine them to form a fifth sentence. Write that sentence in the half circle under the butterfly's head. If extra space is needed , continue the sentence in the bottom half of the circle on the bottom of the butterfly's body.

6. By the end of the exercise, you will have five descriptive sentences created out of ten words and/or phrases.

As a follow-up activity, students can cut out the circles with the sentences in them and place them in a section labeled beginning, middle, or end on a piece of 9-by-18 inch paper. Students must justify why they think the sentence should go under a particular heading.

The Butterfly Helps a Book Discussion Take Wing

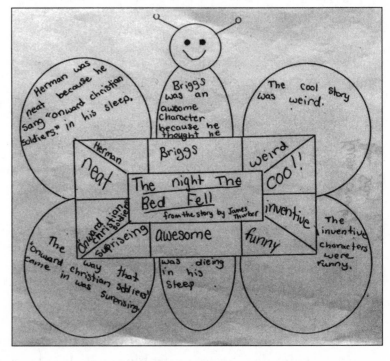

My fourth graders finished reading *The Night the Bed Fell* by James Thurber. I had them work in groups to complete the butterfly graphic. Here is how I directed the lesson:

1. I ask my students to put the name of the story in the center of the graphic.

2. I ask them to describe the story and place their ideas randomly in the boxes around the center. They write: *weird, cool, inventive, funny, awesome, surprising, Onward Christian Soldiers, neat, Herman,* and *Briggs*.

3. I ask them to combine the words in the connected boxes to come up with interesting sentences about the story. Those sentences are placed in the outside circles:

⌧ The cool story was weird.

⌧ The inventive characters were funny.

⊠ The way that "Onward Christian Soldiers" came in was surprising.

⊠ Herman was neat because he sang "Onward Christian Soldiers" in his sleep.

⊠ Briggs was an awesome character because he thought he was dying in his sleep.

The fourth graders found this activity very easy to do. They enjoyed the story and got a kick out of coming up with sentences to describe it. They easily launched into a spirited discussion about the story, further elaborating on their ideas about it.

Fourth Graders Turn Junk Into Gold

My fourth graders are studying inventions. I divide the class into small groups and give each group a pile of junk. They are given 15 minutes to create an invention from their piles of junk. At the end of the activity, each group is given a butterfly graphic organizer. Following are highlights of the activity:

1. *Each group writes the name of their invention in the center box. This group identifies their invention as a "table cleaner."*

2. *In the boxes around the name, students describe their invention and how their invention works. This group identifies their table cleaner as durable, scrubbing sponge, gum pads, retractable, can be pulled, polisher, useful, handles, uses soap and water, and cleans.*

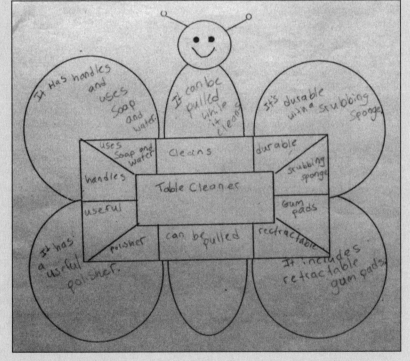

3. *They fill in the circles by combining their ideas from the boxes to form descriptive sentences. The group that invented the table cleaner writes the following:*

   ⊠ *It's durable with a scrubbing sponge.*

   ⊠ *It includes retractable gum pads.*

   ⊠ *It has a useful polisher.*

   ⊠ *It has handles and uses soap and water.*

   ⊠ *It can be pulled while it cleans.*

The groups come together and share their sentences. Most groups have created detailed sentences that describe the function of their inventions.

Flower graphic describes Mosquito Man.

Flower Power

Though a different design, the flower pattern works the same way as the butterfly. The topic to be elaborated upon is placed in the center of the flower. The related ideas are placed in the petals around the center of the flower. The ideas in the petals connected by the larger petals are combined to form one detailed sentence. The sentences are placed in the outer layer of petals.

A fourth grade class invented superheroes to solve local problems. For this class, a superhero named Mosquito Man solves the "crime" of too many mosquitoes. Of course, the superheroes have super powers.

You can see that many ideas have been synthesized to create a more complete description of this superhero. Decisions are made about who this character is before actually writing a sentence about him. Students can use these ideas in a story. Many times, the sentences are just interesting enough to get the students motivated to write.

Second Graders Elaborate

A second grade literacy group used the flower graphic to elaborate on Leviathan, the whale in the story *Kio and Gus*. Everyone in the group had read the story and knew about Leviathan. Because the students used the butterfly graphic organizer many times in the past, they decide they want to try out the flower design.

1. Leviathan is placed in the center circle.

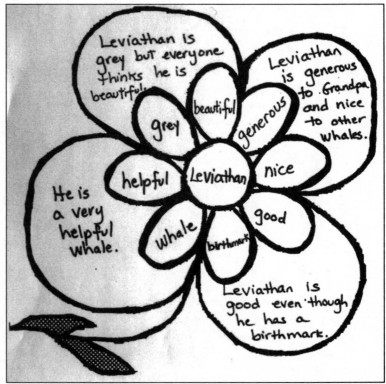

Second graders elaborate on the whale, Leviathan.

54

2. Students generate the following words to describe Leviathan: *generous, nice, good, birthmark, whale, save, awesome, beautiful, gray, helpful.*

3. Students combine the appropriate words to create the following sentences:

- ⊠ Leviathan is generous to Grandpa and nice to other whales.
- ⊠ Leviathan is good even though he has a birthmark.
- ⊠ Leviathan is awesome because he saved Grandpa.
- ⊠ Leviathan is gray, but everyone thinks he's beautiful.
- ⊠ He is a very helpful whale.

After each sentence is generated, students discuss the situation in the story surrounding the idea in the sentence. They justify and verify their statements as they create sentences. The activity is open-ended, allowing for a range in the types of responses. Any sentence is accepted as long as it can be justified through the context of the events in the story.

Some More Tips to Keep in Mind...

▨ The focus of this activity is creativity, because students are synthesizing ideas.

✦ It is more interesting and fun to put seemingly unrelated ideas next to each other. For example, in the Cinderella organizer the words magic and sad do not easily go together. However, this combination encourages creativity and lends itself to more fanciful responses. At first, some students may have difficulty putting two unrelated ideas together. Use your discretion! If this seems too hard at first, then control the location of the words that are placed around the central idea so that it is easy to create sentences. Sentences formed in this way will probably be more predictable and possibly less interesting.

▨ Varied words are challenging but fun. If you and your students really get stuck and have difficulty combining two words, change one of the words in the boxes. Only do this as a last resort to avoid encouraging your students to change words when they are stuck.

✦ If students have difficulty combining the two words, have them think of how attributes of the words are alike. For instance, if students have difficulty combining water and wheel, have them think of how these two concepts and actual words can be alike: both are round, can be clear, begin with "w", can appear and disappear, etc.

▨ If your students don't know how to vary sentence structure, the graphic provides a good opportunity to show them. Tell students to be aware of creating sentences that use the word "is" in them. Explain to students that sentences using the verb "is" are often boring sentences. When building descriptive language, students need to learn the power of the verb.

✦ An idea may be rejected if it does not make sense. For example, when describing Cinderella, if a student says "mean" as a descriptor, ask the student in what way was Cinderella mean. If the student cannot justify the response, do not put the response in the box.

✦ When appropriate, require the students to use vocabulary from a content area as the descriptors. This is a great way for them to practice using their new words in interesting ways.

✦ Decide if you want to do a follow-up activity based on the information generated from the graphic. If you truly want your students to elaborate, then the butterfly or flower graphic organizer does well as a stand-alone acitivity. If you want them to make decisions, prioritize, evaluate information, then extend the activity.

✦ Students will get faster at completing these designs as they become more familiar with the process, but they will slow down if the content is difficult. Generally anticipate it will take your students 15-20 minutes to do this type of activity.

56

Suggested Activities Across the Curriculum

READING WORKSHOP
Adding detail:
- a topic from a nonfiction or fiction story
- a type of story, such as a fairytales
- a character or setting
- two different characters (compare/contrast characteristics)
- a problem

WRITING WORKSHOP
Adding detail:
- forms of poetry
- prewriting activity
- using descriptive language (adjectives only or adverbs only)
- vocabulary building i.e. using vocabulary words
- spelling activity
- integrating sensory writing (descriptors must be sensory words)

MATH WORKSHOP
Elaborate on:
- combining money
- word problems
- adding time
- geometric shapes
- patterns/tessellations
- calendar
- math machine

SOCIAL STUDIES
Elaborate on:
- a concept or theme (our community, change, adaptation, survival)
- a topic
- an explorer
- a place
- a school, community, or global problem
- an event

SCIENCE
Elaborate on:
- life cycles
- food chains
- solar system
- body systems
- wellness
- movement (rotation, reversal)
- environment
- problems in science (recycling, endangered species, pollution)

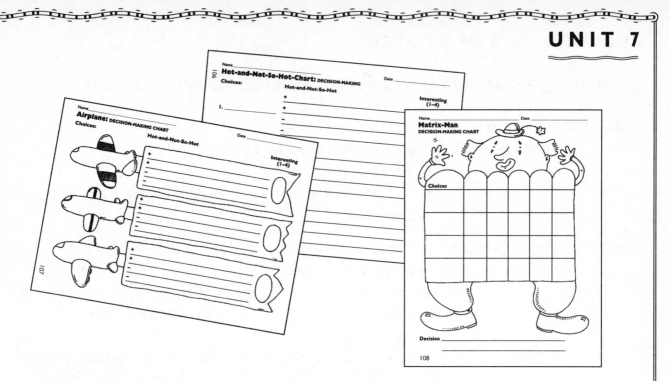

Decision Making Charts

Decision making is an important life skill. It is something we do every day. Students can learn effective decision-making skills by using a structured process. The strategy presented in this unit entails a process involving calculated decision making and high-level critical thinking. Students can learn to analyze a decision in order to make a sound and reasonable evaluation of a situation. This process is not used for simple decision making. It does not utilize spontaneous, reactive thinking. It is used when students need to think about information in depth.

Some students are naturally good at making decisions. They are not fearful of making the wrong decision, the perfect decision, or even the safest decision; however, do they make the most effective decisions? In the following exercises, students use a logical reasoning process to evaluate, justify, and/or confirm their decisions. Students who are good decision makers usually like to use this process, because it complements their natural style and ability.

Some students are not good decision makers. They lack the confidence to make even the simplest determinations. In some cases, this fear may actually impede the learning process. Often, they rely on friends to make decisions for them and become dependent on peer approval. These students might also resort to cheating, lacking the faith in their abilities to answer test questions correctly. The decision-making exercises described in this chapter provide a safety net for these students. They learn to use criteria so they can think through their ideas with more clarity and confidence.

When introducing students to the decision-making process, point out that they are using creative thinking when they consider their choices. They use evaluation when they apply criteria and consider the positives and negatives of each idea.

Group discussion is an important part of group decision making. If a student is making a personal decision, such as what to do during recess, he or she might want to work independently.

Introducing the Hot-and-Not-So Hot-Chart: A MODEL LESSON

Content of the lesson: *Ming Lo Moves the Mountain* by Arnold Lobel

Thinking Skill: Decision making/evaluation

Graphic organizer: Hot-and-not-so-hot chart

The hot-and-not-so-hot chart is derived from psychologist Edward De Bono's concept of what's plus, minus, and interesting about an idea. In the form used here, the words *hot* and *not so hot* identify the good and bad things about an idea. *Interesting* is also used as a descriptor. Here is how I conduct the introductory lesson:

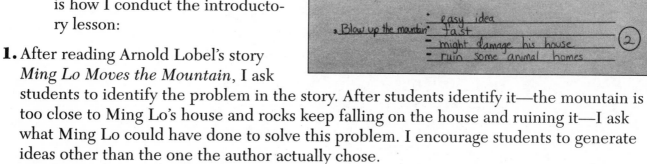

1. After reading Arnold Lobel's story *Ming Lo Moves the Mountain*, I ask students to identify the problem in the story. After students identify it—the mountain is too close to Ming Lo's house and rocks keep falling on the house and ruining it—I ask what Ming Lo could have done to solve this problem. I encourage students to generate ideas other than the one the author actually chose.

2. I ask students to choose their three favorite ideas. (It is best to limit the number of choices when first teaching decision making.)

3. After they have decided upon their three best ideas, I hand out the hot-and-not-so-hot

chart. I ask students to list the three choices next to the numbers one, two, and three.

4. They discuss what is hot about the first idea. They list these ideas next to the plus sign (+). (If students have more than two hot ideas, they can list them on another piece of paper or choose their two favorites.)

5. I lead my students through the same process for the not-so-hot ideas.

6. Before moving on to the second choice, they consider if this first idea is interesting. I remind students not to assess if the idea is effective, realistic, safe, etc., just how *interesting* they find the idea. The hardest part for students to understand is that the most interesting idea is not necessarily the winning idea. Students need to rate how interesting the idea is on a scale of 1-4, with one as the low score and four as the high score.

Hot-and-Not-So-Hot Chart: DECISION MAKING	Ming Lo Loves the Mountain	
Choices:	**Hot-and-Not-So-Hot**	**Interesting (1–4)**
1. Move to a different house	+ new house + – miss his friends – someone may move into his old house and have the same problem.	4
2. Move his house	+ can keep his house + won't have to buy new things – costs a lot money – things might break	3
3. Blow up the mountain	+ easy idea + fast – might damage his house – ruin some animal homes	2

7. I repeat the process for the second and third choices.

8. After analyzing all three choices, I ask students to decide which they like the best. I circle their choice. At this point, each student can make his or her own decision, or I can ask them to make a group decision. I usually let individuals make a decision, unless I'm doing a follow-up activity and all students will need to work from the same response.

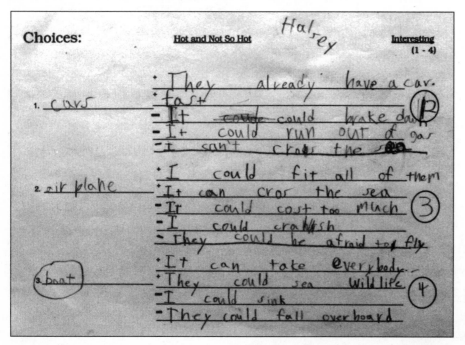

Second grader Halsey Niles made a decision about how Grandpa should travel to Newfoundland, in the story Kio and Gus, *using the hot-and-not-so-hot chart.*

GREAT TEACHING WITH GRAPHIC ORGANIZERS
Scholastic Professional Books, 1998

Introducing the Matrix Man Organizer:
A MODEL LESSON

Content of the lesson: Our community

Thinking skill: Decision making/evaluation

Graphic organizer: Matrix Man

The Matrix Man graphic organizer requires students to weigh sets of criteria for the decisions they make. Explain to students that "criteria" are factors that we consider when making a decision. Model this by giving students examples of generic questions and relating them to key word descriptors. The following are generic criteria that can be used with many decisions:

GENERIC QUESTIONS	KEY WORD DESCRIPTORS
Will it work?	effective
Will it really give me the best results?	results
How long will it take?	time
How much will it cost?	money
How safe is it?	safety
Is it fair?	fair
Do we have the materials/people?	resources
Is it enjoyable?	fun
Is it easy?	easy
Is it useful?	useful

Post the list so students can refer to it. Encourage them to add to the list or generate their own criteria specific to their problems. Once students come up with the criteria, they usually have little or no difficulty rating their ideas. Matrix Man provides a format in which to do this.

Before your students fill one out themselves, walk them through a sample Matrix Man activity. Following are guidelines for an introductory lesson.

1. Make an overhead transparency of the Matrix Man on page 62, and project it on a screen. Tell your class that with this graphic, students were able to set and weigh criteria in order to determine which problem was the most important. Matrix Man provides a format that shows a statistical number which determines the "winning" decision. This graphic is another tool to use when making a logical decision.

2. Point out that students identified four problems in their community: *homelessness, drugs, forest fires,* and *lack of adequate parking spaces.*

3. Next, they brainstormed criteria by which to evaluate the problem. Their criteria are: *leads to crime, affects many people, dangerous to people,* and *costs most to fix.* Notice they do not use generic criteria, and that their criteria is all stated in the negative. Criteria must be stated as either **ALL POSITIVES** or **ALL NEGATIVES**, since you will be using a rating system based on high and low numbers.

4. Students used the first criterion—leads to crime—and rated each idea from 1-4. In this case, the class decided that forest fires lead to the least crime, so they rated it 1. Parking leads to a little more crime, homelessness a little more, and drugs the most. Students must give each choice a different number. They cannot rate the ideas 1,1,2,3. (When introducing second graders to Matrix Man, instead of using numbers, I often have them use smiley faces, frown faces, or a face with a straight mouth on it.)

5. The students used the remaining criteria to rate the problems.

6. The numbers specified in each choice are added across the row and recorded. The highest number determines the winning decision. According to this group of students, the drug problem is considered to be the most important problem that needs to be addressed in their community.

Matrix Man
DECISION-MAKING CHART

Choices	leads to crime	affects many people	dangerous to people	costs most to fix	total
homelessness	3	3	3	4	13
drugs	4	4	4	3	15
forest fires	1	1	2	2	6
parking	2	2	1	1	6

Decision The drug problem is the most important problem to address.

Students used Matrix Man to determine the most important problem in their community.

Clark finds it helpful to use Matrix Man *and the hot-and-not-so-hot chart to help with his decision making.*

Using Both Organizers at Once:
A SAMPLE LESSON

Content of the lesson: Superhero for a foreign country
Thinking skill: Decision making/evaluation
Graphic organizers: Hot-and-not-so-hot chart and Matrix Man

Some students benefit from piggybacking Matrix Man and the hot-and-not-so-hot chart. I have students generate what's hot, not so hot, and interesting about their ideas, and then use their ideas to generate criteria for Matrix Man. This system works really well. For example, fourth graders learned about the United Nations and how countries can come together to promote world peace. As a set-up to a creative writing assignment, students were asked to come up with a superhero who can solve the countries' problems. Clark comes up with three heroes that he likes. He has difficulty deciding which one to use in his creative writing assignment. The teacher asks him to use the decision-making process to help

62

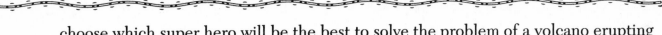

choose which super hero will be the best to solve the problem of a volcano erupting in a country.

1. Clark starts with the hot-and-not-so-hot organizer. He lists his three original superheroes: Cubist, Rainus, and Wah-tor.

2. Cubist can get rid of volcanoes. He uses a funnel that could clog the volcano and keep lava from coming out. The bad things about Cubist are that he is really big and his funnel will remain in the volcano, so lava can come out another time. Clark finds Cubist to be a very interesting character and gives him a 3.7.

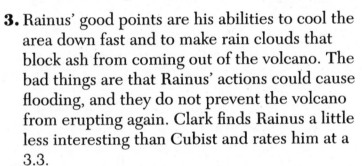

3. Rainus' good points are his abilities to cool the area down fast and to make rain clouds that block ash from coming out of the volcano. The bad things are that Rainus' actions could cause flooding, and they do not prevent the volcano from erupting again. Clark finds Rainus a little less interesting than Cubist and rates him at a 3.3.

4. Wah-tor does not make floods and can put out volcanoes. He does, however, take longer than the others to put out the volcano and his actions do not prevent volcanoes from erupting again. Clark rates Wah-tor as the least interesting hero and gives him a 3.05.

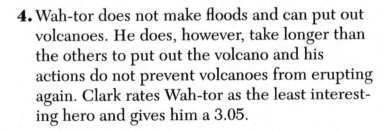

Now, Clark takes the ideas he has generated and uses them in Matrix Man.

1. Clark lists the choices—Wah-tor, Cubist, and Rainus—down the side.

2. He refers to his hot-and-not-so-hot chart for help in choosing criteria. He decides upon *can it erupt again, time, other damage,* and *wildlife damage.*

3. He decides Wah-tor's method is the least effective in stopping the volcano from erupting again. He gives it a one. Rainus' method receives a two, and Cubist gets a three.

4. *Time* refers to how long it takes for the superhero to carry out the plan. Wah-tor's method takes the most time and is rated a one. Cubist is second, and Rainus' method is the quickest and receives a three.

5. Rainus' method does cause other damage, so it receives a one. Wah-tor causes less damage and receives a two. Cubist does not cause other damage and receives a three.

6. Rainus' method causes the most wildlife damage, Cubist less wildlife damage, and Wah-tor causes the least amount of wildlife damage.

7. Clark tallies his numbers and finds that Cubist is the winner. He is happy with his decision. He feels it is well thought out and easy to justify. To conclude the activity, Clark uses his ideas about Cubist to develop a comic strip featuring a super hero who solves problems for his country and saves the day.

Student in the Spotlight

Another group of second graders is asked to decide the best way for the families in *Kio and Gus* to get to Newfoundland. This group uses Matrix Man. For this example, we will focus on the responses of Emma, a student in the group.

1. *Emma's teacher reviews the process of decision making using the Matrix Man format.*

2. *Students list three different ways to get to Newfoundland: plane, train, and car.*

3. *The students generate criteria together. They decide to determine which way is the safest, the most comfortable, the most fun, and the fastest. All of the criteria are a concern for the second graders in the group.*

4. *Individually, students rate each idea according to the criteria. Emma decides that the plane is the least safe, the train is safer, and the car is safest.*

5. *Emma decides the car is the least comfortable, the train is more comfortable, and the plane is the most comfortable.*

6. *Emma decides the car is the least fun, the train is more fun, and the plane is the most fun.*

7. *The car is rated as the least fast, then the train, and the plane is the fastest.*

This second grader used Matrix Man organizer to help the families in Kio and Gus *get to Newfoundland.*

8. *Emma adds up all the plane ratings, the train ratings, and the car ratings and finds the plane has the highest rating. It is determined to be the best idea.*

9. *All the students in this group except one found the plane to be the best idea. That student rated the train highest. In this case, a group decision is not necessary.*

64

Some More Tips to Keep in Mind...

✦ Decision making is a higher-level thinking skill. It incorporates creative thinking when students generate choices and criteria. It uses evaluative thinking when students appraise each idea against set criteria and make a choice.

✖ All students need to learn how to be effective decision makers. This is an important life skill and one that takes practice. The more students are asked to make decisions, the better they will become at decision making.

✦ For those students who say they already know what their decisions are, ask them to go through the process to see if it comes out as they anticipate. Most students will do this to check their answers. As they go through the process, they become aware of the importance of actually thinking over the options before making rash decisions.

✖ Start out with easy decision-making activities. Deciding what to do during a rainy-day indoor recess or deciding on a classroom pet are fairly simple and provide practice for students.

✦ Make sure students know and understand the content that you are asking them to decide about. Students cannot make an informed decision if they are lacking information or content knowledge.

✖ The first time you try this, you might need to list the criteria for students. In the next lesson, you may list a few criteria and students can add their own. Next, students may be asked to generate their own.

✦ By piggybacking the hot-and-not-so-hot organizer with Matrix Man, students can think through their ideas before they put a number value to them.

✖ The hot-and-not-so-hot chart takes about 15 minutes, while Matrix Man takes 20-25 minutes (depending on the difficulty of the decision). Using both graphics together takes over 30 minutes.

✦ When given the choice, students generally prefer to use Matrix Man, not because it is easier, but because they find it more visually appealing.

Suggested Activities Across the Curriculum

READING WORKSHOP
Decide:
- how the story might end
- which is your favorite character
- a way to retell the story
- which story to read next
- how many pages to read each day
- which book you like best
- a title for your story

WRITING WORKSHOP
Decide:
- on a location for your story
- on the best propaganda technique to use in your story
- on a time period for your writing piece
- on the type of poetry you want to use
- on a research topic

MATH WORKSHOP
Decide:
- most useful way we use fractions in real life
- most useful way we use computers
- which math concept we use the most in life
- which container will hold the most fluid
- on a new symbol for money

SOCIAL STUDIES
Decide:
- which is the scarcest resource in the United States
- which city would be the best place to live
- best location for a city playground
- the best thing for a cowboy to do in the 1850s with his little free time
- who is the most valuable community helper
- which president made the most valuable contributions
- which explorer you admire the most

SCIENCE
Decide:
- a course of action for lake clean up
- which is the most appropriate snack
- which is the most effective exercise for getting in shape
- which is the key issue when justifying/criticizing ocean dumping
- safest energy source to use

GREAT TEACHING WITH GRAPHIC ORGANIZERS
Scholastic Professional Books, 1998

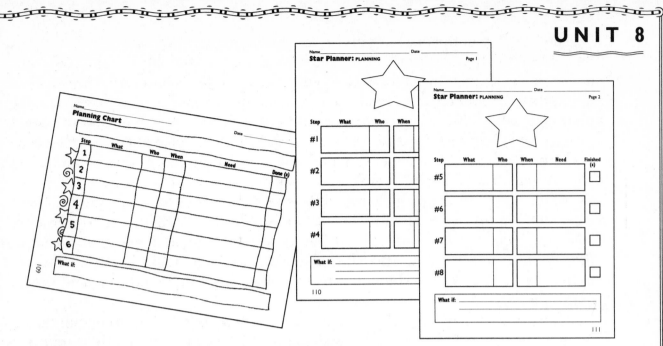

Planning Charts

This chapter presents two different graphic organizers to use with the planning process: the planning chart and the star planner. The planning chart has a box at the top of the page to write what the plan is; the star planner uses a star at the top of the page. The procedures are identical; generally, students are given a choice of which format they prefer. Most students choose the chart, but some consistently choose the star organizer.

Planning is an important organizational skill for you to teach. As dramatic as it may sound, the ability to make a plan and see it through can mean the difference between success and failure in many aspects of life. Students who cannot organize and execute their goals often don't achieve their potential.

When teaching the planning process, establish a shared language so everyone knows and understands the steps in the process. Be sure to teach the process sequentially—unless the steps need to be shortened for a particular reason. Each step is an important part in moving the student from potential to performance.

Point out to students the thinking skills that are involved. To create the plan itself, students use the creative process. They use their powers of analysis throughout, because they need to analyze each step of a plan in order to be successful.

The first step in the planning process is to define what students are planning to do. Sometimes the teacher decides this, and sometimes the students decide. If the students are deciding, they might want to go through the decision-making process first; if not, they sometimes waste as much as half an hour making a decision about what their plan will be. For instance, in one third grade classroom, students were asked to plan a party to commemorate a past U.S. president. Their plan fell apart when they realized they needed to decide whom they were honoring before they could make the plan. A generic plan honoring anyone was not an appropriate response. ·

When using the planning chart and the star planner, students need to decide what happens first, second, third, and so on. For each step, they need to consider *what* will happen, *who* needs to do this, *when* does it need to happen, and what will they *need* in order to do it. After they complete each step, they check off a box next to the step. This gives the students a feeling of accomplishment throughout the entire process.

After students have thought about what each step takes to be successful, they brainstorm what could go wrong. These are called "what ifs." When they brainstorm what ifs, they sometimes realize things they have missed along the way: a step they have forgotten in their plan or perhaps materials they have left out. What ifs give them practice with creative thinking and leave room for them to worry. Tell them now is the time to think about and list all their worries about what could go wrong. By stating their concerns ahead of time, students are more likely to see possible pitfalls before they happen. In this way, they can plan for success.

Introducing the Planning Chart:
A MODEL LESSON

Content of the lesson: Making a mural

Thinking skill: Planning/analysis

Graphic organizer: Planning chart

※ Pass out or project on an overhead a copy of the sample planning chart on page 69. Explain that this graphic organizer can be used to help plan a project or a solution to a problem. Tell them that the sample is from second graders who were planning to make a mural based on the picturebook *One Fine Day*.

※ Show students that the steps to complete this plan are noted by what needs to be done, who will do it, when they will do it, and what they will need in order to do it. Point out step one, which says that the first thing to do is to figure out what needs to be drawn. It is decided that everyone will be needed to do this. They are doing this on Monday. They need a copy of the book, paper, and a marker to do this step.

※ The second step in this plan is to figure out who draws what. Again, everyone is needed to do this, they do it on Monday, and they need a paper and markers to complete this task.

68

The third step is to get the materials. The teacher and a helper will do this on Tuesday. They need mural paper, pencils, erasers and crayons.

The fourth step is to start drawing. Everyone does this on Tuesday and Wednesday. They need mural paper, pencils, erasers, and crayons to do this.

Planning Chart

Make a Mural of *One Fine Day*

Step	What	Who	When	Need	Done (x)
1	Figure out what we will draw	everyone	Mon.	the book, paper, marker	x
2	Figure out who draws what	everyone	Mon.	paper, marker	x
3	get the materials	teacher and helper	Tues.	mural paper, pencils, erasers, crayons	x
4	start drawing	everyone	Tues. & Wed.	mural paper, pencils, erasers, crayons	x
5	clean up	everyone	Tues. & Wed.	trash can	x
6	Hang up our mural	teacher and helper	Wed.	mural, wall, tape	x

What if: everyone doesn't have something to draw?; you have to draw something. you don't know how to draw?; you don't have enough crayons or the right colors?; you don't have enough time to finish your drawing?

Second graders used the planning to chart when they wanted to create a mural for One Fine Day.

The fifth step is to clean up, which everyone does on Tuesday and Wednesday. They need a trash can to do this.

The sixth step in this plan is to hang up the mural. The teacher does this with a helper on Wednesday. They need the mural, a wall, and tape.

The final step is to consider "what ifs." In this case, what if: everyone doesn't have something to draw; you have to draw something you don't really know how to draw; you don't have enough crayons or the right colors; or you don't have enough time to finish your drawing.

After the plan is made, the students in this class follow each step just as they had listed it on the paper. After they complete each step, they make an X in the *done* column.

Explain to your class that these students were very pleased at how their mural came out. They were also proud that they could make a plan and follow it. They liked the process, because it helped them think of everything they needed to do ahead of time, and that helped them to finish on time.

Planning a Trip to Newfoundland

In Unit 7, second graders used decision making organizers to choose a method for the characters in *Kio and Gus* to get to Newfoundland (some chose plane). Now, the students are asked to plan the actual process of taking the plane. After they finish their plan, students read the story to see if the characters actually do take a plane, and if so, the characters' actions match their plan.

Content of the lesson: *Kio and Gus*

Thinking skill: Planning/analysis

Graphic organizer: Planning chart

1. The teacher tells the students that they need to plan the plane trip to Newfoundland.

The students write "take a trip to Newfoundland" in the box at the top of the paper. They agree the first step is to call the airport. They decide Grandpa should do this immediately. He will need a phone, paper, pencil, calendar, and to plan what to say.

2. The next step is to pack. Everyone needs to do this about 48 hours before leaving. They need a suitcase, clothes, a toothbrush, a hairbrush, and toys.

PLANNING

\multicolumn{6}{l}{Take a trip to Newfoundland}					

Steps	What	Who	When	Need	done (X)
1.	Call the airport	Grandpa	Now	Phone, plan what to say Paper, pencil, calendar	✓
2	Pack	us	48 hr before we leave	suitcase Clothes Toothbrush hairbrush Toys	✓
3	Plan trip	us	Now	brochures	✓
4	Leave	us	2 hrs before Plane leaves	Suitcases money tickets	✓
5	Check in	us	1 hour before Plane leaves	suitcase	V
6	Get on the Plane	us	before take off	tickets	✓

What if: Plane breaks? Plane is delayed by weather? We lose our tickets?

3. The next step is to plan their vacation time while in Newfoundland. Everyone is going to do this together as soon as they get brochures.

4. They all need to leave about two hours before the plane leaves. They need to remember to take their suitcases.

5. They all need to check in when they get to the airport. They need their suitcases when they do this.

6. They all need to get on the plane just before it takes off. They need their tickets to do this.

7. The students in the group generate the following what if questions: What if the plane breaks; What if the plane is delayed by bad weather; or What if we lose our tickets?

The students are so excited about their plan, they can hardly wait to read the story to see if it actually happens this way. Let's look at the same lesson using the star planner. Notice that the responses are similar but do vary slightly.

70

Content of the lesson: *Kio and Gus*

Thinking skill: Planning

Graphic organize: Star planner

1. The teacher tells the students they need to plan the plane trip to Newfoundland. They are asked to write "take a plane to Newfoundland" in the star, because that is what they are planning to do. They agree the first step is to call the airport for information and to book the flight. They decide Grandpa will do this immediately. He will need the phone number, phone, paper, and pencil. As the students agree on the responses, the teacher writes the answers on the board. The students copy them on their paper.

2. They decide the next thing to do is pack. Everybody needs to do this the day before leaving. They decide they need a suitcase, clothes, toothbrush, and playthings.

PLANNING

Take a plane to Newfoundland

	Who	What	When	Need	Finished
Step #1	Kio's Grandpa	Call airport for information	Now	phone number, phone, paper + pencil	☑
#2	everybody	Pack	day before leaving	Clothes Suitcase toothbrush Play-things	☑
#3	everybody	Go to airport	1 hour before plane leaves	suitcases money Car	☐
#4	adults	Take out Suitcases Buy tickets (check in)	↑ Same	Cart Suitcases tickets	☑

What if: We don't have enough money? We miss the plane? We don't have enough Suitcases? We could forget something!

3. The next step is to go to the airport. Everyone does this one hour before the plane leaves. They need the suitcases, money, and the car.

4. The fourth step is to check in at the airport. They need to take out the suitcases and get their boarding passes. The adults do this one hour before the plane leaves. They need the suitcases, a cart to carry the suitcases, and the tickets.

5. Notice that the star planner is only numbered one through four. At this point students need a second paper numbered five through eight. For step five, students decide everybody needs to get on the plane. They do this just before the plane leaves. They need everybody to do this; they also need the tickets.

6. In the last step, everybody gets off the plane in Newfoundland. They do this when the plane stops, and they need everything they brought.

Notice that the group using the planning chart end their plan when the families get on the plane. The group using the star planner end their plan when the families get off the plane. Of course, either resolution is correct. The second group was so thorough in their planning process that they actually felt like the family really did arrive in Newfoundland. It was amazing to see them visualize the process.

Some More Tips to Keep in Mind...

- ✦ Planning is a higher-level thinking skill that involves analysis, evaluation, and decision making; however, the plan itself involves the creative process, as students develop a creative plan.

- ✠ Plans may be used to promote creativity. For instance, in the case of the class that read *Kio and Gus*, the students planned a trip for the family in the story. When they finished reading the story, they found out that the family did not take a plane at all. The author did not choose to write the story the way the students imagined it.

- ✦ Plans may be used to solve problems or work out social situations. For instance, plan how to solve the problem of fights on the playground. Students will begin to see that a planning process exists in all aspects of life and is available to them any time they need it. They will also be more comfortable following a plan than they would a list of rules.

- ✠ Start out with group plans, so that students know and understand each step of the process. Planning seems like an easy process to learn. It is the actual carrying out of the plan that is difficult. It takes practice for students to learn to set realistic goals and time frames. Also, developmentally, younger children have little sense of how long things take to do. Help them make realistic plans so that they can be successful.

- ✦ Let students know that anytime they take materials out, they must put them away. Both steps should be listed on their plan.

- ✠ It is motivating for students to make a plan and actually carry it out. In this way, they get immediate feedback. They realize where their plans fall short, or they realize how thoroughly they have thought out their projects. They learn to become good planners.

- ✦ It is dangerous to use a planning graphic organizer every time students need to make something. Plans should be used for longer projects that involve many steps or long time frames.

- ✠ Plans are generally easy for students to use. If they have something fairly simple to plan out, the process takes about 10-15 minutes. The more complex the task, the longer it takes the students to figure out all the steps and complete their plans.

GREAT TEACHING WITH GRAPHIC ORGANIZERS
Scholastic Professional Books, 1998

Suggested Activities Across the Curriculum

READING WORKSHOP
Plan:
- a presentation about the book you just read
- a diorama showing a scene from the story
- a puppet show
- to put together a book project
- to summarize specific aspects of the story
- to illustrate a theme in a short story

WRITING WORKSHOP
Plan:
- how to improve journal entries
- how to write an essay
- an interview of a family member
- a photographic essay or book
- a display for your best writing piece

MATH WORKSHOP
Plan:
- the best way to learn the times tables
- to set a goal in math and make a plan for it
- to set up a school store
- a computer activity
- to make a math game
- a research project on a mathematician

SOCIAL STUDIES
Plan:
- a birthday celebration for the United States
- to make a map of our town
- a model of an island
- to research a country
- a celebration to honor the famous outlaws of the 1800's
- an imaginary trip in 1890 on the Oregon trail

SCIENCE
Plan:
- how to save energy at home/school
- a science project
- to present ideas about healthy snacks in a skit
- a wildlife mask
- a model of the solar system
- to build an invention
- a debate on the pros and cons of zoos

Integrating Graphic Organizers

This section shows the many ways graphic organizers can be integrated into a unit of study. The content of the unit is identified and the graphic organizers are listed with ideas for lessons.

ANIMALS

COMPARE AND CONTRAST ORGANIZER

- compare and contrast mammals and reptiles
- compare and contrast places where different animals live
- compare and contrast animals and their predators
- compare and contrast two kinds of wild animals

CAUSE/EFFECT WEB

- what would happen if more animals became extinct
- causes and effects of lack of places to hibernate
- what would happen if animals had no fur
- what would happen if it were illegal to have pets

FORECASTING CHART

- analyze problems related to endangered species
- analyze problems related to the need for animals to adapt to their environment
- analyze problems related to finding food in the winter
- analyze problems of health issues such as allergies and family pets

DRAWING CONCLUSIONS CHART

- draw conclusions about a wolf
- draw conclusions about an elephant
- draw conclusions about an animal rights group
- draw conclusions about the rights of animals

CREATIVE THINKING CHART

- think of many, different ways to combine two animals to come up with a new animal
- think of many, different things a Panda could eat
- think of many, different birthday presents you could give a giraffe
- think of many, different ways to persuade your mom or dad to let you have a pet

ADDING DETAIL ORGANIZER

- describe a monkey (characteristics of an animal)

GREAT TEACHING WITH GRAPHIC ORGANIZERS
Scholastic Professional Books, 1998

⊠ describe eucalyptus leaves (an animal's food source)

⊠ describe a bear's cave (an animal's home)

⊠ describe a mammal's characteristics

DECISION MAKING CHART

⊠ decide on the best animal to have as a classroom pet

⊠ decide which endangered animal you think is the most important to save

⊠ decide which wild animal is the most dangerous

⊠ decide which domestic animal is the cutest

PLANNING CHART

⊠ plan a report on your favorite animal

⊠ plan a skit about African animals

⊠ plan a diorama showing a scene of an animal hibernating

⊠ plan to make a mask representing an endangered animal

SIMPLE MACHINES

COMPARE AND CONTRAST ORGANIZER

⊠ compare and contrast levers and pulleys

⊠ compare and contrast types of levers

⊠ compare and contrast a wedge and a lever

⊠ compare and contrast a gear and a clock

CAUSE/EFFECT WEB

⊠ what would happen if gears had never been invented

⊠ what would happen if all levers were made of wood

⊠ what would happen if we had no axles and wheels

⊠ causes and effects of simple machines

FORECASTING CHART

⊠ analyze the problems related to the increase in the number of machines

⊠ analyze the problems of machines doing the jobs people used to do

⊠ analyze the problems related to people operating heavy machinery

⊠ analyze the problems of using simple machines

DRAWING CONCLUSIONS CHART

⊠ draw conclusions about a lever

⊠ draw conclusions about a pulley

⊠ draw conclusions about the jobs simple machines can do

⊠ draw conclusions about a person who discovers a simple machine

CREATIVE THINKING CHART

⊠ think of many, different ways to combine two simple machines

⊠ think of many, different ways to use a screw

⊠ think of many, different ways to improve a lever

⊠ think of many, different things a pulley could pull

ADDING DETAIL ORGANIZER

⊠ describe a simple machine

⊠ describe force

⊠ describe fulcrum

⊠ describe how your body is like a machine

DECISION MAKING CHART

⊠ decide which simple machine is the most useful

⊠ decide which simple machine to use to move a big rock

⊠ decide which simple machine you would like to play with

⊠ decide which simple machine you will try to make

PLANNING CHART

⊠ plan to make a simple machine that performs a specific task

⊠ plan to present a skit about a simple machine

⊠ plan a chart to show how machines help us

⊠ plan a field trip to visit a machine shop

EXPLORERS

COMPARE AND CONTRAST ORGANIZER

⊠ compare and contrast two explorers

⊠ compare and contrast a past and a present explorer

⊠ compare and contrast an ocean explorer and a space explorer

⊠ compare and contrast the explorer in the story with another character in the story

CAUSE/EFFECT WEB

⊠ what would happen if Europeans had not discovered the "New World"

⊠ what would happen if there weren't any maps

⊠ what would happen if there were no such thing as explorers

⊠ what would happen if explorers were not brave

FORECASTING CHART

☒ analyze problems related to using inaccurate maps

☒ analyze the problems of the effects of long sea voyages

☒ analyze the problems of communication between explorers and settlers

☒ analyze the problems of exploring new territory

DRAWING CONCLUSIONS CHART

☒ draw conclusions about Christopher Columbus

☒ draw conclusions about Marco Polo

☒ draw conclusions about the spice trade

☒ draw conclusions about the problem of expensive Eastern goods

CREATIVE THINKING CHART

☒ think of many, different ways weather affects exploration

☒ think of many, different places to explore

☒ think of many, different things to take with you on an exploration

☒ think of many, different uses for a map

ADDING DETAIL ORGANIZER

☒ describe an explorer

☒ describe the Northwest Passage

☒ describe merchants

☒ describe Columbus' ships

DECISION MAKING CHART

☒ decide which explorer had the biggest impact on your life

☒ decide where was the most unusual place Marco Polo visited

☒ decide which expedition was the most dangerous

☒ decide who got the most recognition for a discovery

PLANNING CHART

☒ plan a celebration to honor an explorer

☒ plan a research report about an explorer

☒ plan a birthday card to send to your favorite explorer

☒ plan a mural depicting a scene from an exploration

OUR COMMUNITY

COMPARE AND CONTRAST ORGANIZER

- ⊠ compare and contrast two types of communities
- ⊠ compare and contrast two kinds of community services
- ⊠ compare and contrast two community helpers
- ⊠ compare and contrast two community problems

CAUSE/EFFECT WEB

- ⊠ what would happen if there were no fire people
- ⊠ what would happen if nobody volunteered in our community
- ⊠ causes and effects of our trash disposal system
- ⊠ what would happen if there was no crime in our community

FORECASTING CHART

- ⊠ analyze a problem related to pollution
- ⊠ analyze the biggest problem in our community
- ⊠ analyze the homeless problem in our community
- ⊠ analyze a problem in our school

DRAWING CONCLUSIONS CHART

- ⊠ draw conclusions about the population growth in our community
- ⊠ draw conclusions about the history of our community
- ⊠ draw conclusions about the natural resources in a community
- ⊠ draw conclusions about leadership roles in a community

CREATIVE THINKING CHART

- ⊠ think of many, different ways we can get people to care about their community
- ⊠ think of many, different new jobs that could become part of a community
- ⊠ think of many, different solutions to a problem in a community
- ⊠ think of many, different government structures for a community

ADDING DETAIL ORGANIZER

- ⊠ describe your community
- ⊠ describe community resources
- ⊠ describe community jobs
- ⊠ describe community helpers

DECISION MAKING CHART

- ⊠ decide which is the most important job in a community

GREAT TEACHING WITH GRAPHIC ORGANIZERS
Scholastic Professional Books, 1998

- decide the type of community you would like to live in
- decide one thing that you would like to change in your community
- decide one thing that you would bury in a time capsule for people to find in future years that would represent your community

PLANNING CHART

- plan a new playground for your park
- plan a new school
- plan a way to volunteer in your community
- plan to visit the nursing home

HUMAN BODY

COMPARE AND CONTRAST ORGANIZER

- compare and contrast two body parts
- compare and contrast health issues today and the 1900s
- compare and contrast the digestive system and the nervous system
- compare and contrast eating healthy and not eating healthy

CAUSE/EFFECT WEB

- what would happen if we had no sense of sight
- what would happen if there was no such thing as disease
- what would happen if health care was free
- what would happen if someone discovered the fountain of youth

FORECASTING CHART

- analyze a problem related to health care
- analyze a problem related to exercise
- analyze the problem of losing one of the senses
- analyze the problem of drugs and sports

DRAWING CONCLUSIONS CHART

- draw conclusions about a famous person who invented a cure for something
- draw conclusions about a particular disease
- draw conclusions about the respiratory system
- draw conclusions about the use of medicine

CREATIVE THINKING CHART

- think of many, different ways to compensate for the loss of hearing
- think of many, different parts to add to the body to make it work better

- think of many, different ways to stay healthy
- think of many, different ways to teach someone about the human body

ADDING DETAIL ORGANIZER
- describe the brain
- describe the heart
- describe the circulatory system
- describe wellness

DECISION MAKING CHART
- decide which body system is the most mistreated
- decide which playground rule provides you with the most safety
- decide which sense you think would be the worst to lose
- decide which is the biggest health issue right now

PLANNING CHART
- plan a way to inform the public about health issues
- plan a balanced diet
- plan to make a model of the muscular/skeletal system
- plan a healthy snack for the class

RAIN FOREST

COMPARE AND CONTRAST ORGANIZER
- compare and contrast two of the layers of the rain forest
- compare and contrast two endangered animals that live in the rain forest
- compare and contrast the rain forest today and the rain forest of years ago
- compare and contrast the rain forest and a regular forest environment

CAUSE/EFFECT WEB
- what would happen if the rain forest destruction continues
- causes and effects of endangered animals in the rain forest
- what would happen if the canopy area was missing
- what would happen if nobody was ever allowed in a rain forest

FORECASTING CHART
- analyze a problem related to the rain forest
- analyze a problem related to trying to save the endangered species
- analyze the problem of cutting trees in the rain forest
- analyze the problem of using plants from the rain forest as medicine

GREAT TEACHING WITH GRAPHIC ORGANIZERS
Scholastic Professional Books, 1998

DRAWING CONCLUSIONS CHART

- ⊠ draw conclusions about the rain forest
- ⊠ draw conclusions about the orangutan
- ⊠ draw conclusions about the jaguar
- ⊠ draw conclusions about a lifestyle without rubber products

CREATIVE THINKING CHART

- ⊠ think of many, different ways to save the rain forest
- ⊠ think of many, different uses for rain forest plant products
- ⊠ think of many, different examples of beauty that could be found in the rain forest
- ⊠ think of many, different sounds you might hear in the rain forest

ADDING DETAIL ORGANIZER

- ⊠ describe the rain forest
- ⊠ describe the layers of the rain forest
- ⊠ describe the weather in the rain forest
- ⊠ describe the location of rain forests

DECISION MAKING CHART

- ⊠ decide which is the most important endangered species to save
- ⊠ decide the best way to save the rain forest
- ⊠ decide the best way to protect animal habitats in the rain forest
- ⊠ decide upon a new law that would protect the rain forest

PLANNING CHART

- ⊠ plan a trip to a rain forest
- ⊠ plan a story using rain forest animals in it
- ⊠ plan to read the story *Under the Kapote Tree*
- ⊠ plan to make an original game that would teach others about the rain forest

TRANSPORTATION

COMPARE AND CONTRAST ORGANIZER

- ⊠ compare and contrast trains and planes
- ⊠ compare and contrast planes and jets
- ⊠ compare and contrast influences of transportation in the early 1900s to now
- ⊠ compare and contrast different types of boats

CAUSE/EFFECT WEB

- ⊠ what would happen if cars had never been invented

GREAT TEACHING WITH GRAPHIC ORGANIZERS
Scholastic Professional Books, 1998

☒ what would happen if all cars ran on solar power

☒ what would happen if there was no such thing as private transportation

☒ what would happen if everyone had their own planes

FORECASTING CHART

☒ analyze the growth problem related to the transportation industry

☒ analyze the fuel source problem

☒ analyze the safety problem in the transportation industry

☒ analyze the pollution problem

DRAWING CONCLUSIONS CHART

☒ draw conclusions about General Motors Company

☒ draw conclusions about solar powered cars

☒ draw conclusions about the Wright Brothers

☒ draw conclusions about the *Titanic*

CREATIVE THINKING CHART

☒ think of many, different modifications to make a car better

☒ think of many, different new kinds of transportation

☒ think of many, different problems that overcrowded airports need to deal with

☒ think of many, different safety features for a particular type of transportation

ADDING DETAIL ORGANIZER

☒ describe a hand glider

☒ describe a hydrofoil

☒ describe a monorail

☒ describe a blimp

DECISION MAKING CHART

☒ decide which type of transportation is the most important in your community

☒ decide which problem is the most important problem to solve in the transportation industry

☒ decide which energy source you would like to see used in the future

☒ decide the most significant influence of transportation

PLANNING CHART

☒ plan a transportation system for the future

☒ plan a model of your future form of personal transportation

☒ plan a report on the history of transportation

☒ plan a skit demonstrating the effects of transportation on the city

GREAT TEACHING WITH GRAPHIC ORGANIZERS
Scholastic Professional Books, 1998

SOLAR SYSTEM

COMPARE AND CONTRAST ORGANIZER

- ⊠ compare and contrast two planets
- ⊠ compare and contrast two astronauts
- ⊠ compare and contrast planets and stars
- ⊠ compare and contrast a solar system and a galaxy

CAUSE/EFFECT WEB

- ⊠ what would happen if a space object spins out of its rotation
- ⊠ what would happen if you were chosen to be the next astronaut
- ⊠ what would happen if there was no such thing as gravity
- ⊠ what would happen if the Earth stopped rotating

FORECASTING CHART

- ⊠ analyze a problem that NASA faces
- ⊠ analyze a problem with space exploration
- ⊠ analyze a problem with charting the universe
- ⊠ analyze a problem with public support for space exploration

DRAWING CONCLUSIONS CHART

- ⊠ draw conclusions about how patterns in the solar system influence our lives
- ⊠ draw conclusions about the existence of patterns in the solar system
- ⊠ draw conclusions about the time differences between living on Earth and living on Mars
- ⊠ draw conclusions about the existence of other galaxies

CREATIVE THINKING CHART

- ⊠ think of many, different things you would take with you in space
- ⊠ think of many, different things you could see in space
- ⊠ think of many, different ways to build a model of our solar system
- ⊠ think of many, different characteristics of space objects

ADDING DETAIL ORGANIZER

- ⊠ describe a space object
- ⊠ describe a comet
- ⊠ describe a meteor
- ⊠ describe space pollution

DECISION MAKING CHART

- ⊠ decide who you would take with you to colonize a planet
- ⊠ decide what you would do if you met another life form
- ⊠ decide how often space shuttles should be sent up in space
- ⊠ decide what is the most important characteristic an astronaut should possess

PLANNING CHART

- ⊠ plan to find out how much money the United States spends on space exploration
- ⊠ plan to write a letter to an astronaut
- ⊠ plan to make a model of the solar system
- ⊠ plan to show how an eclipse works

FAIRY TALES: Jack and the Beanstalk

COMPARE AND CONTRAST ORGANIZER

- ⊠ compare and contrast Jack and the Giant
- ⊠ compare and contrast the magic beans and the magic harp
- ⊠ compare and contrast Jack's house and the Giant's house
- ⊠ compare and contrast Jack and his mother

CAUSE/EFFECT WEB

- ⊠ what would happen if the beans were not magical
- ⊠ what would happen if the Giant sued Jack for stealing his things
- ⊠ what would happen if Jack and his mother had jobs
- ⊠ what would happen if Jack only dared to go up the beanstalk once

FORECASTING CHART

- ⊠ analyze Jack's problem of disappointing his mother
- ⊠ analyze the Giant's problem of not being able to see too well
- ⊠ analyze the Giant's problem of having someone sneak into his house
- ⊠ analyze Jack's problem of being greedy

DRAWING CONCLUSIONS CHART

- ⊠ draw conclusions about Jack
- ⊠ draw conclusions about the Giant
- ⊠ draw conclusions about the harp
- ⊠ draw conclusions about Jack's mother

CREATIVE THINKING CHART

- ⊠ think of many, different ways Jack could pay the giant back

84

- think of many, different ways the story could end
- think of many, different things you would say to Jack if you met him
- think of many, different designs for the Giant's house

ADDING DETAIL ORGANIZER

- describe Jack
- describe the goose
- describe the Giant
- describe Jack's house

DECISION MAKING CHART

- decide what Jack should do with all the Giant's things
- decide whom Jack's mother marries
- decide what Jack did with the beanstalk leaves that were all over the ground after he cut the beanstalk down
- decide how old Jack is in the story

PLANNING CHART

- plan a feast for Jack and his mother
- plan a letter from the Giant to Jack
- plan a holiday called Beanstalk Day
- plan to make a video reenacting the story

FAIRYTALES: Cinderella

COMPARE AND CONTRAST ORGANIZER

- compare and contrast Cinderella with her stepsisters
- compare and contrast the fairy godmother and the Prince
- compare and contrast Cinderella's house and the Prince's castle
- compare and contrast the mice and the horses

CAUSE/EFFECT WEB

- what would happen if there was no fairy godmother
- causes and effects of Cinderella working hard
- causes and effects of the stepsisters being mean to Cinderella
- what would happen if the story of Cinderella took place today

FORECASTING CHART

- analyze the problem of Cinderella wanting to go to the ball
- analyze the problem of Cinderella having to leave the ball at midnight

❉ analyze the problem of the Prince having to find Cinderella

❉ analyze the problem of Cinderella living in the country

DRAWING CONCLUSIONS CHART

❉ draw conclusions about the Prince

❉ draw conclusions about Cinderella's animal friends

❉ draw conclusions about the fairy godmother

❉ draw conclusions about the setting of the story

THE CREATIVE THINKING CHART

❉ think of many, different ways Cinderella could have gotten to the ball if there had been no fairy godmother.

❉ think of many, different ways Cinderella could thank her fairy godmother

❉ think of many, different uses for Cinderella's glass slipper

❉ think of many, different designs for Cinderella's wedding dress

ADDING DETAIL ORGANIZER

❉ describe how it felt for Cinderella to dance with the Prince

❉ describe how the stepsisters felt when they discovered the beautiful girl at the dance was Cinderella

❉ describe how Cinderella might have felt when she moved into the palace

❉ describe Cinderella's feelings toward animals

DECISION MAKING CHART

❉ decide who will be Cinderella's maid or matron of honor

❉ decide where Cinderalla and the Prince will go on their honeymoon

❉ decide the perfect wedding gift for Cinderella and the Prince

❉ decide the name of Cinderella and the Prince's favorite song

PLANNING CHART

❉ plan a dramatization of the castle wedding

❉ plan a model of the castle

❉ plan to make swords, crowns, scepter, and capes for the dramatization

❉ plan wedding invitations

GREAT TEACHING WITH GRAPHIC ORGANIZERS
Scholastic Professional Books, 1998

Try It...You'll Like It!

Through this book, I hope you have discovered some graphic organizers you are eager to try. Remember: If one graphic organizer doesn't seem to work, go ahead and modify it. These are flexible tools designed to be used in a variety of ways. Let's take a look at some commonly asked questions.

How do I get started using graphic organizers?

1. Identify the content.

2. Select a graphic organizer that can be used to enhance the learning of the content.

3. Show a sample graphic organizer, or show how it works.

4. Have the students try the graphic organizer using the content of the lesson. They can do this with you, in a small group, or on their own, depending on the age of the students and the complexity of the content.

5. Have students share responses.

6. The graphic organizer may be the product of the lesson, or students can use the ideas they generate as information for a follow-up activity.

7. The responses listed in a graphic organizer may or may not be assessed.

How often should I go over how a graphic organizer works before I can expect my students to be able to do it on their own?

The graphic organizers presented in this book are simple formats. After seeing once or twice how the format works, most students will be able to complete an organizer with little teacher guidance. When students have difficulty, consider if it is because of the organizer or a lack of content information. Usually, students have more trouble with content than they do with the organizers. If this is the case, make sure the content of the lesson is easy enough for all students to be able to respond to successfully.

What about my student who doesn't like to write?

A graphic organizer is a wonderful tool for students who don't like to write or have difficulty writing. Many of the graphic organizers do not require students to write whole sentences, just one or two words. I allow students who won't write at all to draw responses. This, of course, takes more time and more space. This option is available to the students only some of the time. Think about how you help a nonwriter in any writing activity. Use the same technique when using graphic organizers requiring written responses.

What about my nonverbal students? How will I know what the student knows if we are doing a graphic organizer together and the students are responding orally?

It is important to vary the type of responses so that all learners can be accommodated. Written, visual, or hands-on responses would work best for the nonverbal student.

How often should I use graphic organizers? Won't my students get tired of applying information this way?

Graphic organizers are motivational. I usually use graphic organizers once or twice a week. They are fun and easy to use. Make sure you vary the types of graphics you use. Students should be so familiar with their structures that they can actually use them on their own outside of school.

How do I manage the class when they are doing these in small groups?

If students are working in small groups, the class can become noisy. Usually students are engaged, and they are discussing responses. Move from group to group, and make sure they are on task. Remind them to talk softly so that other groups do not hear their responses until it is time to share.

What if the lesson doesn't work? What if I get stuck?

Consider what part of the lesson isn't working. Is it the match between the type of graphic organizer and the content of the lesson? Do the students have enough information about the content to respond? Do the students remember the information? Is it a match between the student and the type of graphic organizer? Have you asked a student who is very analytical to do an activity that is mostly creative? Have you allowed enough time? When you figure out why the lesson does not work, you will be more successful next time. In the meantime, you may stop the lesson and let students know the lesson is not working out the way you had planned. Then go ahead and rework the lesson in a different way. It is okay for students to see you try something and make a mistake. You are actually modeling how to try something and not be perfect at it the first time. This is a wonderful lesson for the perfectionists in your class.

What if I don't like one of the graphic organizers?

There has been a lot of information released regarding styles. There are learning styles, cognitive styles, personality styles, etc. Notice how you might be drawn to graphics that utilize creative thinking. You might find you like the ones that are analytical. And then there is format style. You might like the ones that are linear. You might like the ones that are whole pictures or have a random pattern. Just because you like particular strategies does not mean that everyone will like the same ones. Try to use the ones you like and the ones you don't like. That way you will make all your students happy.

What about evaluation and record keeping?

Remember, you don't have to evaluate every activity a student does. If you feel the need to evaluate, make sure the students do the work individually. A group grade is generally not representative of each individual's knowledge. When using the graphic organizer as the end product, students need to know that their responses will be graded.

As for record keeping, it is helpful to observe the activity and jot down notes regarding a particular student's performance. Unusual responses, excitement, degree of engagement in the activity, and success with the graphic organizer is important

GREAT TEACHING WITH GRAPHIC ORGANIZERS
Scholastic Professional Books, 1998

information to share with parents or to help you when developing a profile of the student. It is also important to pinpoint who is making little success.

I also like to keep track of the types of graphic organizers students choose. If a student always chooses a cause/effect web, I know the student probably likes the way this strategy is structured. The student also may prefer to do cause/effect thinking. I can watch to see how often the student chooses to use this strategy, and I encourage the student to branch out.

What about letting students create their own graphic organizers?

Students will naturally modify graphics to fit their needs. They add, delete spaces, add shapes, and sometimes come up with an original organizer. Some of the graphic organizers presented in this book were designed, modified, or inspired by young students. As long as the graphic works, we use it. The more formats we have, the more variety is available.

A FINAL WORD

All of the formats presented in this book have been field tested in classrooms. They have proven to be effective teaching tools that can be used with all students in many different content areas. They are used to enhance students' understanding of content and higher-level thinking skills. They provide interactive flexible formats that are motivating and fun for students. Start by choosing a graphic organizer that appeals to you, and use it with your students until you feel they are ready to learn how to use another one.

As soon as you are comfortable using graphic organizers, you will see how most lessons can be taught by using a graphic organizer format. The trick is to just get started. Just try one...I think you will like it.

Bug: COMPARE AND CONTRAST

Name_____ Date _____

Caterpillar: COMPARE AND CONTRAST

Hens: COMPARE AND CONTRAST

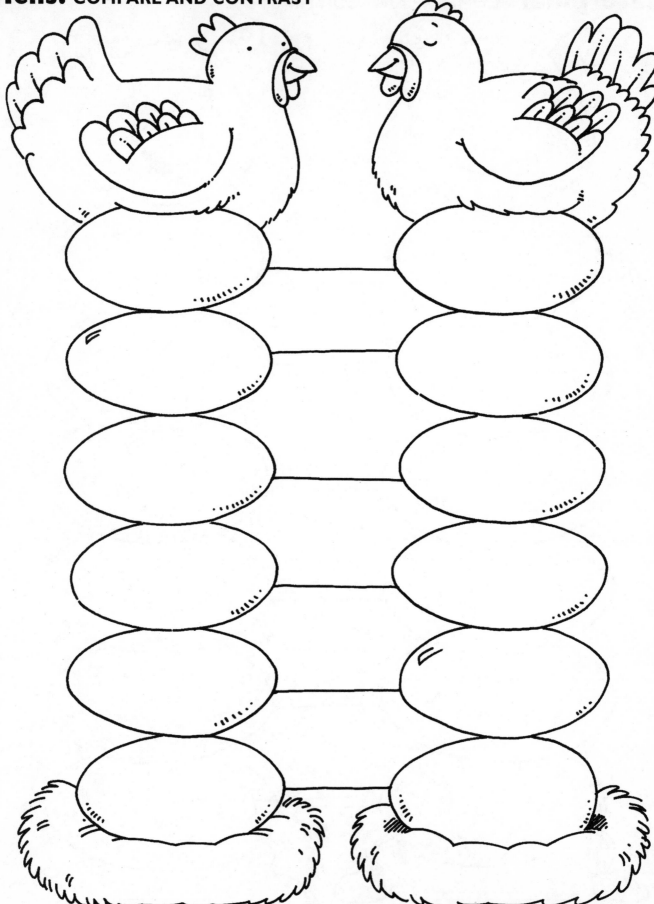

GREAT TEACHING WITH GRAPHIC ORGANIZERS
Scholastic Professional Books, 1998

Flappers: COMPARE AND CONTRAST

_____   _____

Cause and Effect Web

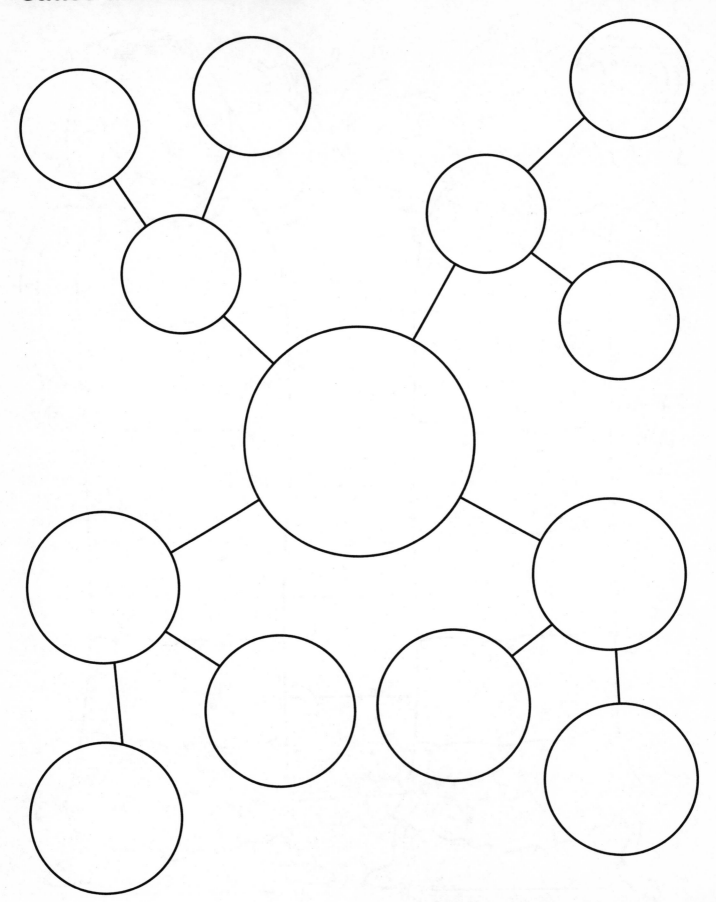

GREAT TEACHING WITH GRAPHIC ORGANIZERS
Scholastic Professional Books, 1998

Cause and Effect Web

Name_____ Date _____

Forecasting Chart

TOPIC OR CONCEPT

Issues/ Problems

Issue/Problem

Resulting Effects or Consequences

Trend/Problem

Resulting Effects or Consequences

Consequence

Alternatives to Prevent Consequence

Alternative

Action Plan

GREAT TEACHING WITH GRAPHIC ORGANIZERS
Scholastic Professional Books, 1998

Drawing Conclusions Chart

Verb: SUPPORTING

Procedure:

1. Choose a character or topic.
2. List general statements that describe the character or topic.
3. Choose one general statement.
4. List evidence to support the statement in your own words.
5. Cite sources to prove evidence.
6. Present conclusion in paragraph form.

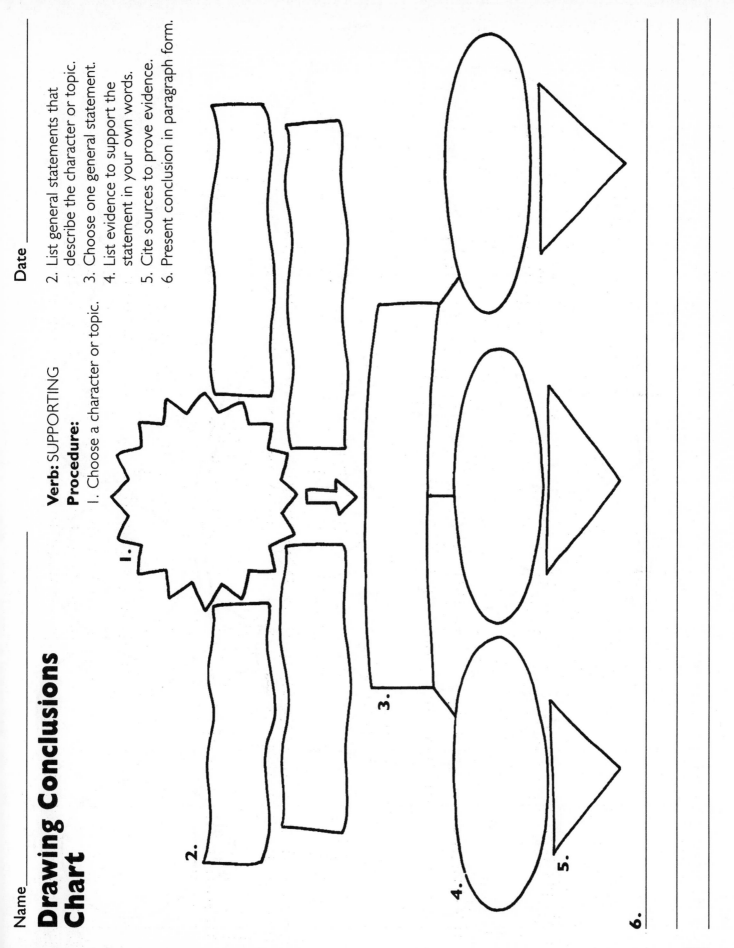

1.

2.

3.

4.

5.

6.

Turtle: CREATIVE THINKING

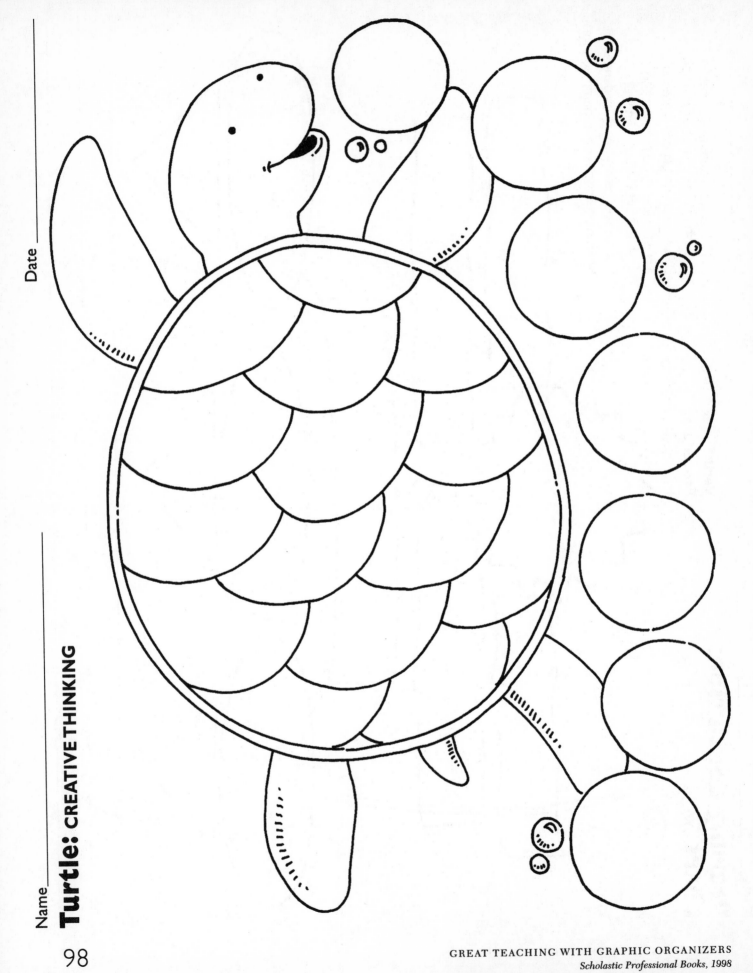

GREAT TEACHING WITH GRAPHIC ORGANIZERS
Scholastic Professional Books, 1998

Pot of Gold: CREATIVE THINKING

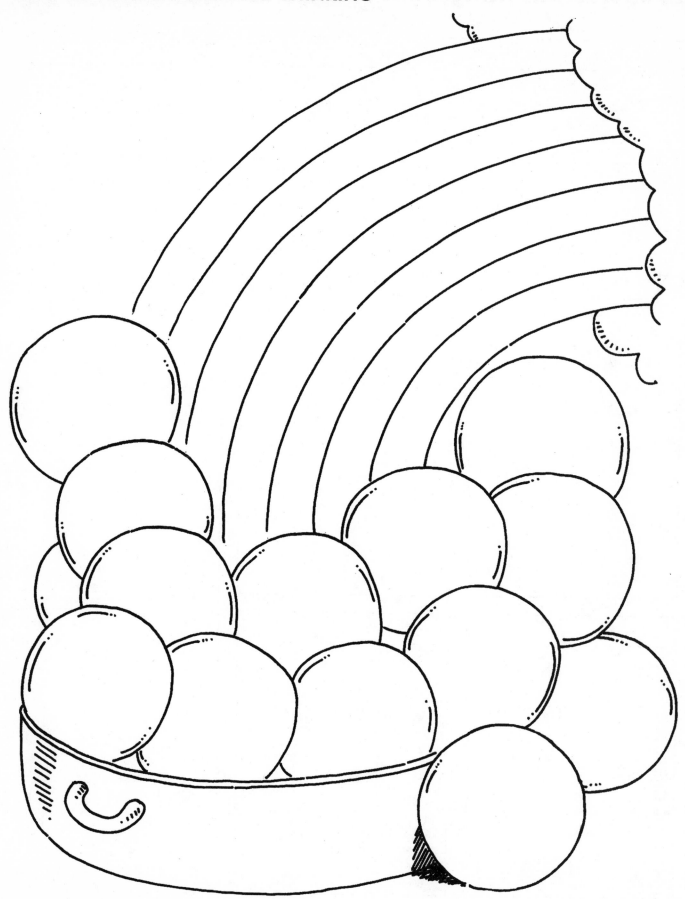

Creative Thinking Chart

_____

_____

☐ _____   ☐ _____

☐ _____   ☐ _____

☐ _____   ☐ _____

☐ _____   ☐ _____

☐ _____   ☐ _____

GREAT TEACHING WITH GRAPHIC ORGANIZERS
Scholastic Professional Books, 1998

Creative Thinking at the Cream Soda Cafe

Name _____

Butterfly: ADDING DETAIL

GREAT TEACHING WITH GRAPHIC ORGANIZERS
Scholastic Professional Books, 1998

Flower: ADDING DETAIL

Skater: ADDING DETAIL

GREAT TEACHING WITH GRAPHIC ORGANIZERS
Scholastic Professional Books, 1998

The Bed: ADDING DETAIL

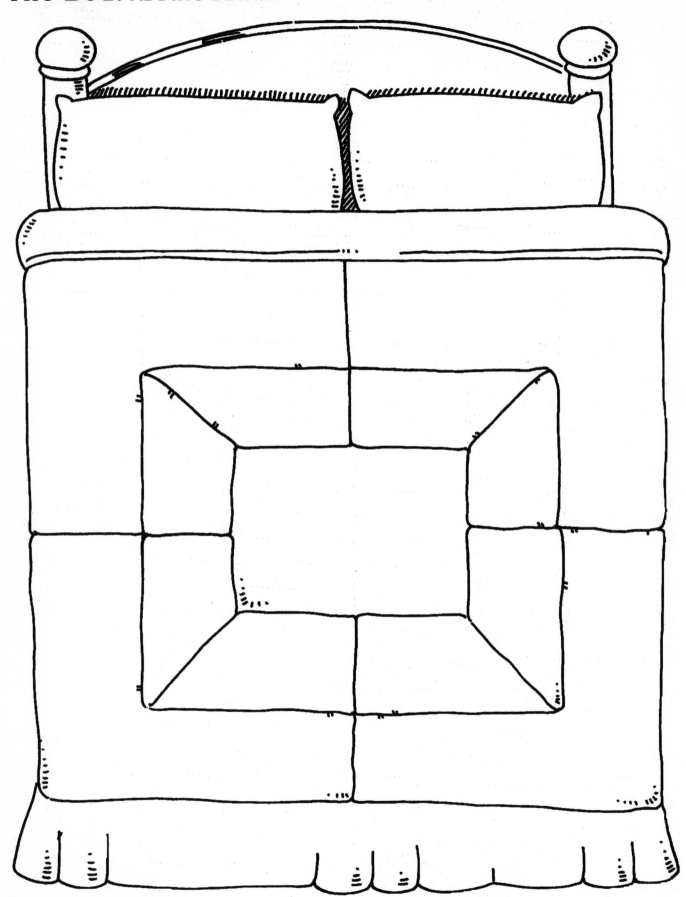

Name _____

Date _____

Hot-and-Not-So-Hot Chart: DECISION MAKING

Interesting (1–4)

Hot-and-Not-So-Hot

Choices:

1. _____

2. _____

3. _____

+ + ‒ ‒   + + ‒ ‒   + + ‒ ‒

GREAT TEACHING WITH GRAPHIC ORGANIZERS
Scholastic Professional Books, 1998

Name _____

Date _____

Airplane: DECISION MAKING CHART

**Interesting
(1–4)**

Hot-and-Not-So-Hot

Choices:

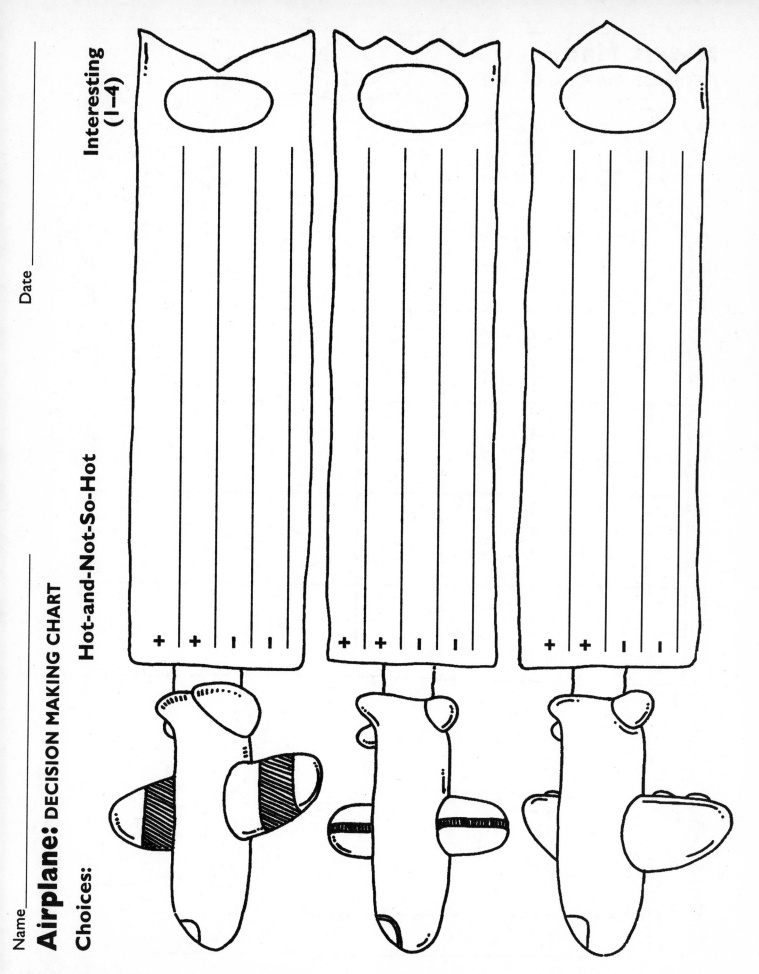

Name_____ Date _____

Matrix Man
DECISION MAKING CHART

Choices

Decision _____

_____

GREAT TEACHING WITH GRAPHIC ORGANIZERS
Scholastic Professional Books, 1998

Name _____

Date _____

Planning Chart

Step	What	Who	When	Need	Done (x)
1					
2					
3					
4					
5					
6					

What if:

Name_____ Date _____

Star Planner: PLANNING

Step	What	Who	When	Need	Finished (x)
#1					☐
#2					☐
#3					☐
#4					☐

What if: _____
_____
_____

GREAT TEACHING WITH GRAPHIC ORGANIZERS
Scholastic Professional Books, 1998

Name_____ Date _____

Star Planner: PLANNING

Step	What	Who	When	Need	Finished (x)
#5					☐
#6					☐
#7					☐
#8					☐

What if: _____
_____

Professional Resources

Balsamo, K. (1994). *Thematic Activities for Student Portfolios*. Beavercreek, OH: Pieces of Learning.

Bellanca, J. (1990). *The Cooperative Think Tank: Graphic Organizers to Teach Thinking in the Cooperative Classroom*. Arlington Heights, IL: IRI/Skylight.

Black, H. & Black, S. (1990). *Organizing Thinking: Graphic Organizers*. Pacific Grove, CA: Midwest Publications.

Bromley, K., Vitis, L., & Modlo M. (1995). *Graphic Organizers*. New York: Scholastic.

de Bono, Edward. (1968). *New Think*. New York: Avon

Fogarty, R., & Bellanca, J. (1991). *Patterns for Thinking: Patterns for Transfer*. Palatine, IL: Skylight Publishing

Helfgott, D., Helfgott, M. & Hoof, B. (1994). Inspiration software: The Visual way to quickly develop and communicate ideas. Portland, OR: Inspiration software

Heyerle, D. (1995). *Thinking Maps: Tools for Learning*. Cary, NC: Innovative Sciences.

Heyerle, D. (1996). *Visual Tools for Constructing Knowledge*. Alexandria, VA: Association for Supervision and Curriculum Development.

Margulies, N. (1991). *Mapping Innerspace*. Tucson, AZ: Zephyr Press.

O'Brien-Palmer, Michelle. (1997). *Great Graphic Organizers to Use With Any Book*. New York: Scholastic.

Parker, J. (1989). *Instructional Strategies for Teaching the Gifted*. Boston, MA: Allyn and Bacon.

Parks, S. & Black, H. (1989 & 1992). *Organizing Thinking: Graphic Organizers, Book I & II*. Pacific Grove, CA: Midwest Publications.

Wycoff, J. (1991). *Mindmapping: Your Personal Guide to Exploring Creativity and Problem Solving*. New York: Berkley Books.